SELLING FOR RESULTS

THE HEALTH CLUB GUIDE TO PROFESSIONAL SELLING

SELLING FOR RESULTS

THE HEALTH CLUB GUIDE TO PROFESSIONAL SELLING

BY BRENDA ABDILLA

CBM
BOOKS
Cardinal Business Media Inc.

The information in this book is subject to change without notice and should not be construed as a commitment by the author or the publisher. Although every precaution has been taken in the preparation of this book, the publisher assumes no responsibility for errors or omissions.

Printed in the United States of America

Library of Congress Cataloging-in-Publication Data

Abdilla, Brenda, 1962 --
      Selling for results: the health club's guide to professional
      selling/by Brenda Abdilla
      p. cm.
      includes Index
      ISBN 1-878956-65-5
      1. Physical fitness centers -- United States -- Marketing.
      I. Title.
      GV429.A35   1996
      796'.06'8--dc20   96-14020
                         CIP

Please address comments and questions to the publisher:
CBM Books
1300 Virginia Drive, Suite 400
Fort Washington, PA 19034
(215) 643-8000 FAX (215) 643-8099
http://www.cardinal.com/cbmbooks

Editor: Grace Palsgrove
Production Manager: Laura LoMonaco Derr
Typesetting: Richard Lowden

DEDICATION

To every salesperson out there
spending your days
selling your heart out.
It is an honor to be part of your team.

TABLE OF CONTENTS

BEFORE YOU BEGIN

Like many salespeople, the first thing I ever excelled at in life was selling. I was an average performer in almost everything I tried in grade and high school. Having terrible asthma as a child, I didn't get involved in sports until my adolescence, a bit late to become an Olympic hopeful in gymnastics. In school, teachers said I was bright, but a bit too talkative. Imagine that! I had a pretty good singing voice and went to the state championships with my choir group, but lacked the discipline to pursue it. I had a lot of determination but I was not a star at anything.

During one summer, when I was not quite 14, one of my older girlfriends got a summer job telemarketing for an aluminum siding and insulation company. The company needed more part-time help and she asked her boss if I could have the job. I begged my mom to let me have the job—it would require her dropping me off and picking me up for my four-hour shifts, five days a week. She gave in. The job consisted of cold calling people at home and selling them on an appointment to have an "energy consultant" visit their home and give them a free estimate. I averaged two hundred appointments per week and broke every target and record the company ever set. I didn't know it then, but I had found my life's passion and career—selling!

From that summer on, every job I've had in one way or another turned into a sales position. When I was waiting tables to pay for my college tuition, I usually sold the finest wine and had the highest ticket average. When I worked as a bank teller, the president of the large bank chain created a position for me selling specialized services right in the bank lobby. When I was an aerobics instructor for a studio chain called Richard Simmon's Anatomy Asylum, I quickly learned that all instructors sold memberships when not teaching class. Only then did I start to appreciate the profession of selling and consider myself a real salesperson.

Of all of my titles, professional speaker, consultant, and so on, the one I identify the most with is salesperson. That's what I know the most about—selling and salespeople. That's what I am. If that's what you are or want to be, you may find this book very helpful. I have taken what I have learned in almost 14 years in the health and fitness industry and boiled it down to what works best. Similar to my seminars, I don't like to waste words or talk theory. You will find the information to the point and practical. On that note, let's get started.

HOW TO GET THE MOST OUT OF THIS BOOK

The book begins with a brief test to uncover your true sales philosophy. Many philosophies to selling a product exist. Although there is no absolute right or wrong philosophy to selling, there certainly is a general direction that will serve you better than others might.

The rest of the book is divided into three sections.

The first section covers the process of selling a membership, from the introduction all the way through to the addressing of objections. Each chapter will help you change some typical bad habits made in that step and will give you some good habits to replace them. Each chapter in Section 1 also contains an easy script to follow and practice.

Section 2 consists of only one chapter, Mastering the Incoming Call, and it deals with the important issue of handling business that comes to you. True mastery on the telephone is a difficult task to achieve, but it can be done. This chapter comes after the selling process instead of before because it deals with complicated issues like how not to give pricing over the phone and dealing with obnoxious callers—issues I felt would be easier to learn once you had the main selling ideas committed to memory.

Section 3 deals with generating your own business; one of our industries most over-emphasized subjects. Approaching small, medium and even large companies is easier than you think. I share with you a program that I began developing more than 10 years ago while I called on companies in many different markets. My hope is that Section 3, Chapter 7, will help you become an independent salesperson instead of dependent on the telephone to ring.

I would encourage you to learn verbatim the scripts and language used in the book. People have a tendency to read or hear something and then to immediately add their own style to it. Try learning it first and then add your personal touch. It usually takes a little time for the real meaning of the words or language to sink in. Try memorizing it first. That way you can add your own style without losing any of the desired effect.

I hope you enjoy reading this book as much as I enjoyed writing it.

WHAT IS YOUR SELLING PHILOSOPHY?

The following test is designed to help you uncover your personal selling philosophy. Don't worry about scoring well. This is not a skills test, it's a philosophy test. The test is for you and results should be kept confidential.

Often times, we develop our sales philosophy from other people without even realizing that our beliefs are not our own. In other cases, we are forced to act a certain way when selling because our work environment dictates it.

This is an opportunity to find out what your beliefs are about selling memberships and the first step toward making any needed changes.

There are 60 questions in the three sections below. Make a check next to the description that most accurately reflects your response to the statement made. Be honest!

SECTION 1

Check one response for each statement below:

1. I am a one-call closer. I don't let 'em get away.

    5 ___ Strongly agree

    4 ___ Agree

    0 ___ Don't know if I agree or disagree

    2 ___ Disagree

    1 ___ Strongly disagree

2. I close as many times as I can during the selling process. Closing is the name of the game.

    5 ___ Strongly agree

    4 ___ Agree

    0 ___ Don't know if I agree or disagree

    2 ___ Disagree

    1 ___ Strongly disagree

3. I just keep closing and closing and closing.

   5 ___ Strongly agree

   4 ___ Agree

   0 ___ Don't know if I agree or disagree

   2 ___ Disagree

   1 ___ Strongly disagree

4. Sometimes prospects need a little shocker like "I was under the impression that you wanted to really work on your physical appearance."

   5 ___ Strongly agree

   4 ___ Agree

   0 ___ Don't know if I agree or disagree

   2 ___ Disagree

   1 ___ Strongly disagree

5. I like to write the prices out during my price presentation instead of working with a printed rate card. That way I can fully explain the options.

   5 ___ Strongly agree

   4 ___ Agree

   0 ___ Don't know if I agree or disagree

   2 ___ Disagree

   1 ___ Strongly disagree

6. I enjoy doing T.O.s (turning the prospect over to someone else) because it can be an effective way to close an uncertain prospect.

   5 ___ Strongly agree

   4 ___ Agree

   0 ___ Don't know if I agree or disagree

   2 ___ Disagree

   1 ___ Strongly disagree

7. I find that "...If I could, would you?" statements are very effective in gaining commitment from a prospective buyer.

   5 ___ Strongly agree

   4 ___ Agree

0 ___ Don't know if I agree or disagree

2 ___ Disagree

1 ___ Strongly disagree

8. The close is the most important part of the selling process!

   5 ___ Strongly agree

   4 ___ Agree

   0 ___ Don't know if I agree or disagree

   2 ___ Disagree

   1 ___ Strongly disagree

9. I like to put the prospects on the equipment during the tour to involve them more in the process.

   5 ___ Strongly agree

   4 ___ Agree

   0 ___ Don't know if I agree or disagree

   2 ___ Disagree

   1 ___ Strongly disagree

10. Most people don't know what they should or shouldn't be doing. The tour gives me a chance to tell about the club and share some knowledge with the person.

    5 ___ Strongly agree

    4 ___ Agree

    0 ___ Don't know if I agree or disagree

    2 ___ Disagree

    1 ___ Strongly disagree

11. I always list all of the features of the club and do so on the phone and on the tour.

    5 ___ Strongly agree

    4 ___ Agree

    0 ___ Don't know if I agree or disagree

    2 ___ Disagree

    1 ___ Strongly disagree

12. I do the same tour because I have my technique down pat like a pro. I have built trial closes and test questions into my tour.

5 ___ Strongly agree

4 ___ Agree

0 ___ Don't know if I agree or disagree

2 ___ Disagree

1 ___ Strongly disagree

13. I get most prospects to commit to an exercise program (or the product) before I will even show them the club. I get them to say it.

5 ___ Strongly agree

4 ___ Agree

0 ___ Don't know if I agree or disagree

2 ___ Disagree

1 ___ Strongly disagree

14. Selling is a numbers game.

5 ___ Strongly agree

4 ___ Agree

0 ___ Don't know if I agree or disagree

2 ___ Disagree

1 ___ Strongly disagree

15. I find out the needs of prospects by asking them very frank questions about their exercise history, current program and how they feel about themselves and the shape they're currently in. If people were happy with themselves they wouldn't be here.

5 ___ Strongly agree

4 ___ Agree

0 ___ Don't know if I agree or disagree

2 ___ Disagree

1 ___ Strongly disagree

16. I sometimes use very direct questions to help people see their own patterns of failure.

5 ___ Strongly agree

4 ___ Agree

0 ___ Don't know if I agree or disagree

2 ___ Disagree

1 ___ Strongly disagree

17. I start out all of my interactions with a big smile and strong welcome. I am a take-charge person who is excited about my product and it shows. This helps me get psyched up to make a sale.

5 ___ Strongly agree

4 ___ Agree

0 ___ Don't know if I agree or disagree

2 ___ Disagree

1 ___ Strongly disagree

18. I am not very good at the paperwork part of selling. I am a motivator and a talker. Leave the paperwork to the losers!

5 ___ Strongly agree

4 ___ Agree

0 ___ Don't know if I agree or disagree

2 ___ Disagree

1 ___ Strongly disagree

19. My leads are generally scattered all over the desk. This helps me to sell better because it makes me feel busy.

5 ___ Strongly agree

4 ___ Agree

0 ___ Don't know if I agree or disagree

2 ___ Disagree

1 ___ Strongly disagree

20. The reality is that sometimes selling requires withholding certain information from buyers—not super-important information, just details that would sometimes distract the buyer.

5 ___ Strongly agree

4 ___ Agree

0 ___ Don't know if I agree or disagree

2 ___ Disagree

1 ___ Strongly disagree

Total points Section 1 _____

SECTION 2

Check one response for each statement below:

1. People can decide for themselves without being closed. I can read people and most of them don't like being pushed.

   5 ___ Strongly agree

   4 ___ Agree

   0 ___ Don't know if I agree or disagree

   2 ___ Disagree

   1 ___ Strongly disagree

2. I never really get objections from people because I never really ask them to buy.

   5 ___ Strongly agree

   4 ___ Agree

   0 ___ Don't know if I agree or disagree

   2 ___ Disagree

   1 ___ Strongly disagree

3. I always let people try the club (product) first. That way they can really tell if it's for them or not.

   5 ___ Strongly agree

   4 ___ Agree

   0 ___ Don't know if I agree or disagree

   2 ___ Disagree

   1 ___ Strongly disagree

4. I like helping people, not necessarily selling to them.

   5 ___ Strongly agree

   4 ___ Agree

   0 ___ Don't know if I agree or disagree

   2 ___ Disagree

   1 ___ Strongly disagree

5. Clearly, the most important part of the selling process is the tour.

   5 ___ Strongly agree

   4 ___ Agree

   0 ___ Don't know if I agree or disagree

   2 ___ Disagree

   1 ___ Strongly disagree

6. My tours are the longest part of the selling process. People have a right to know what they are buying. I give a great club tour.

   5 ___ Strongly agree

   4 ___ Agree

   0 ___ Don't know if I agree or disagree

   2 ___ Disagree

   1 ___ Strongly disagree

7. I try to let the prospects control the interaction so that they will feel more comfortable with me.

   5 ___ Strongly agree

   4 ___ Agree

   0 ___ Don't know if I agree or disagree

   2 ___ Disagree

   1 ___ Strongly disagree

8. I find most salespeople obnoxious. I personally don't like to deal with salespeople when I am making a purchase.

   5 ___ Strongly agree

   4 ___ Agree

   0 ___ Don't know if I agree or disagree

   2 ___ Disagree

   1 ___ Strongly disagree

9. I feel that all people have a right to go home and think about their purchase before buying.

   5 ___ Strongly agree

   4 ___ Agree

   0 ___ Don't know if I agree or disagree

2 ___ Disagree

1 ___ Strongly disagree

10. I am a much better salesperson in person versus on the telephone.

5 ___ Strongly agree

4 ___ Agree

0 ___ Don't know if I agree or disagree

2 ___ Disagree

1 ___ Strongly disagree

11. I feel that it is inappropriate to call people at their workplace.

5 ___ Strongly agree

4 ___ Agree

0 ___ Don't know if I agree or disagree

2 ___ Disagree

1 ___ Strongly disagree

12. I feel intrusive calling people anytime but I do it because it is part of my job.

5 ___ Strongly agree

4 ___ Agree

0 ___ Don't know if I agree or disagree

2 ___ Disagree

1 ___ Strongly disagree

13. I never have to ask for referrals.

5 ___ Strongly agree

4 ___ Agree

0 ___ Don't know if I agree or disagree

2 ___ Disagree

1 ___ Strongly disagree

14. My leads are completely organized. I spend a great deal of time getting and staying organized. My work space is clean and orderly most of the time.

5 ___ Strongly agree

4 ___ Agree

0 ___ Don't know if I agree or disagree

2 ___ Disagree

1 ___ Strongly disagree

15. I generally work the hours I am scheduled to work. I am efficient and do not find it necessary to work beyond my normal hours.

5 ___ Strongly agree

4 ___ Agree

0 ___ Don't know if I agree or disagree

2 ___ Disagree

1 ___ Strongly disagree

16. I do not have a sales background. I sort of fell into this position.

5 ___ Strongly agree

4 ___ Agree

0 ___ Don't know if I agree or disagree

2 ___ Disagree

1 ___ Strongly disagree

17. I am involved in many aspects of the club besides selling memberships.

5 ___ Strongly agree

4 ___ Agree

0 ___ Don't know if I agree or disagree

2 ___ Disagree

1 ___ Strongly disagree

18. I do not really think of myself as a salesperson but more of a customer service person.

5 ___ Strongly agree

4 ___ Agree

0 ___ Don't know if I agree or disagree

2 ___ Disagree

1 ___ Strongly disagree

19. I do most of my prospecting and customer work through the mail. I am constantly sending things to people. I have a good system for this.

5 ___ Strongly agree

4 ___ Agree

0 ___ Don't know if I agree or disagree

2 ___ Disagree

1 ___ Strongly disagree

20. I am sometimes amazed at what people spend on memberships.

5 ___ Strongly agree

4 ___ Agree

0 ___ Don't know if I agree or disagree

2 ___ Disagree

1 ___ Strongly disagree

Total points Section 2 _____

SECTION 3

Check one response for each statement below:

1. I make at least 20 outgoing calls each day to potential members and referrals, regardless of how I feel or how busy I am.

5 ___ Strongly agree

4 ___ Agree

0 ___ Don't know if I agree or disagree

2 ___ Disagree

1 ___ Strongly disagree

2. I force myself to do my lead tracking because I like to see what my ratios are.

5 ___ Strongly agree

4 ___ Agree

0 ___ Don't know if I agree or disagree

2 ___ Disagree

1 ___ Strongly disagree

3. I am honored to be in the profession of selling and I use books and tapes to help me learn more and stay focused.

   5 ___ Strongly agree

   4 ___ Agree

   0 ___ Don't know if I agree or disagree

   2 ___ Disagree

   1 ___ Strongly disagree

4. My favorite part of the selling process is finding out the needs. I find closing to be almost effortless when I have done a good job at uncovering the needs.

   5 ___ Strongly agree

   4 ___ Agree

   0 ___ Don't know if I agree or disagree

   2 ___ Disagree

   1 ___ Strongly disagree

5. Even though I am an enthusiastic communicator I force myself to listen closely to people. I find that each person has come in for a reason unique to himself or herself. This makes selling much more interesting.

   5 ___ Strongly agree

   4 ___ Agree

   0 ___ Don't know if I agree or disagree

   2 ___ Disagree

   1 ___ Strongly disagree

6. I always briefly sit down with prospects before showing them around the club. If they are really aggressive, I just stand still and ask the questions, but I always ask questions to find out needs and interests before proceeding.

   5 ___ Strongly agree

   4 ___ Agree

   0 ___ Don't know if I agree or disagree

   2 ___ Disagree

   1 ___ Strongly disagree

7. I maintain control of the entire interaction with the prospective members without being pushy or aggressive. I concentrate entirely on them and their needs, but I am in control.

5 ___ Strongly agree

4 ___ Agree

0 ___ Don't know if I agree or disagree

2 ___ Disagree

1 ___ Strongly disagree

8. I am careful to pay attention to the level of comfort of the prospects. If they seem uncomfortable I will usually diffuse it. Discomfort can be diffused if handled right.

5 ___ Strongly agree

4 ___ Agree

0 ___ Don't know if I agree or disagree

2 ___ Disagree

1 ___ Strongly disagree

9. I do a very brief, customized tour. I feel that more is not necessarily better when it comes to showing the club.

5 ___ Strongly agree

4 ___ Agree

0 ___ Don't know if I agree or disagree

2 ___ Disagree

1 ___ Strongly disagree

10. I take the prospects to the area of most interest first. I sometimes even tell them the monthly rate on the tour just to prepare them for the price presentation.

5 ___ Strongly agree

4 ___ Agree

0 ___ Don't know if I agree or disagree

2 ___ Disagree

1 ___ Strongly disagree

11. I know every little idiosyncrasy of my club (like not enough parking) and have a rational answer or option for them all. I have researched and practiced each one and can answer each honestly but I do not act apologetically for any aspect of our facility.

   5 ___ Strongly agree

   4 ___ Agree

   0 ___ Don't know if I agree or disagree

   2 ___ Disagree

   1 ___ Strongly disagree

12. Not only do I never lie to my prospective members, but I sometimes correct them on a mistaken assumption that could cause me to lose the sale. I figure better now than later.

   5 ___ Strongly agree

   4 ___ Agree

   0 ___ Don't know if I agree or disagree

   2 ___ Disagree

   1 ___ Strongly disagree

13. My closing questions are totally customized to the type of person I am dealing with. I like closing.

   5 ___ Strongly agree

   4 ___ Agree

   0 ___ Don't know if I agree or disagree

   2 ___ Disagree

   1 ___ Strongly disagree

14. I ask 100 percent of my tours to buy a membership.

   5 ___ Strongly agree

   4 ___ Agree

   0 ___ Don't know if I agree or disagree

   2 ___ Disagree

   1 ___ Strongly disagree

15. I never try to intimidate or patronize the prospects when they have an objection. Objection handling is easy if you stay calm, pause a little and ask some good questions.

    5 ___ Strongly agree

    4 ___ Agree

    0 ___ Don't know if I agree or disagree

    2 ___ Disagree

    1 ___ Strongly disagree

16. I can ask people almost anything once we have developed a rapport. I let them do the talking and I ask the questions.

    5 ___ Strongly agree

    4 ___ Agree

    0 ___ Don't know if I agree or disagree

    2 ___ Disagree

    1 ___ Strongly disagree

17. I am a goal setter. I have written goals for everything that is important to me in my life.

    5 ___ Strongly agree

    4 ___ Agree

    0 ___ Don't know if I agree or disagree

    2 ___ Disagree

    1 ___ Strongly disagree

18. I am excellent on the telephone. I have really worked to develop the skills for both outgoing and incoming calls. Nobody is a "natural" on the phone—it takes skill.

    5 ___ Strongly agree

    4 ___ Agree

    0 ___ Don't know if I agree or disagree

    2 ___ Disagree

    1 ___ Strongly disagree

19. I am not a big fan of paperwork, but I do it quickly and efficiently and move on to the parts of my job I love.

5 ___ Strongly agree

4 ___ Agree

0 ___ Don't know if I agree or disagree

2 ___ Disagree

1 ___ Strongly disagree

20. I am a calm, polished, educated, professional salesperson who just happens to be passionate about health and fitness. I could probably get a job selling in the corporate environment, but I prefer this industry.

5 ___ Strongly agree

4 ___ Agree

0 ___ Don't know if I agree or disagree

2 ___ Disagree

1 ___ Strongly disagree

Total points Section 3 _____

RECORD YOUR SCORES HERE:

Total score for Section 1 _____

Total score for Section 2 _____

Total score for Section 3 _____

In my seven years of travels as a professional sales trainer, I have found that salespeople in the health club industry generally fall into one of three categories when it comes to their sales philosophy and belief system:

1. THE OLD SCHOOL OR TRADITIONAL SELLING SYSTEM

(Those who score 40 or above in Section 1).

This philosophy essentially boils down to closing, closing and closing. The most obvious of the three selling styles, it can sometimes feel manipulative to the salesperson and the prospect. The old school is the way I learned to sell, 14 years ago. It is based on the basic assumption that people, if left to their own devices, will not make a purchase without being somehow maneuvered.

It is also based on the win/lose principle. Somebody has to win and somebody has to lose in order for the interaction to be successful. It's only natural that the salesperson wants to be the winner and is therefore expected to say or do whatever it takes to make sure that he or she wins. This philosophy is still quite prevalent in our industry and can be effective on the surface.

The problems with this type of selling arise on more of a subconscious level. Even though the person may have purchased a membership, on some level they know they were mishandled or pressured. The member may retaliate when it comes time for them to tell their friends about your business or may overreact when the club disappoints them in some small way. The best reason to reconsider your answers to the questions in Section 1 is that you can be effective without this type of selling. Our society is much more sensitive to this type of selling and it is clear that traditional salespeople who can't seem to change turn people off. The automobile industry is a classic example of the traditional selling reputation.

2. THE CUSTOMER SERVICE APPROACH OR NON-SELLING ATMOSPHERE
(Those who scored 40 or above in Section 2).

This philosophy was born in an effort to not use the traditional or old school approach. The problem is that it is often taken too far in our industry. In an effort not to seem pushy or too forward some salespeople totally relinquish control to the prospect. This interaction has almost no chance of going well because the wrong person is in charge. Often due to an anti-selling philosophy on the part of the manager or owner, salespeople who use this style can come off as weak and timid in the eyes of the prospect. Another reason a person may have this philosophy is because he or she may have been promoted from the fitness department and has a belief that selling is bad or manipulative, by nature. The only way to address this is through good sales training that focuses on the needs instead of manipulation techniques. Selling is an honorable profession and done professionally, can really make a difference in the lives of others. Most clubs have already figured out that very few businesses in today's competitive marketplace can survive without the use of the selling process.

3. THE NEED BASED SELLING SYSTEM OR PROFESSIONAL SELLING
(Those who scored 80 or above in Section 3).

This philosophy, I feel, takes the best aspect of the traditional selling approach and the customer service approach. It is definitely selling, yet does not have many of the aspects that can turn buyers off. This philosophy is based on the principle of win/win. If the prospect wins, the business wins. This philosophy combines honesty with sales techniques, two items that were mutually exclusive in the early days of our industry. This system is based on the assumption that people are interested in your product and are more likely to become customers and stay customers if they are treated like adults. A professional salesperson takes control of the interaction without condescending the buyer or using obvious techniques, yet he or she does discover the needs and asks closing questions just as a real salesperson should. My sense is that everyone involved in this process feels better about it than they do with either of the above methods and attitudes.

The test was divided into three sections (instead of being mixed-up) so that you could become aware of your own behaviors and attitudes as you re-read the questions. Ideally, you want the lowest possible score you can achieve in Sections 1 and 2 and the highest possible score in Section 3. If you scored about the same in each section, you may have been trying to psyche out the test. Go back and answer again to see if your score comes out differently.

SELLING SECRETS OF TOP PRODUCERS IN THE FITNESS INDUSTRY

I love the telephone and spend about 70% of my day on it.

I am vicious about my time and what I do with it.

I sell on needs versus interests.

I am stingy with guest passes and giveaways.

I don't negotiate with negotiators.

I know my ratios.

I don't buy into low expectations set by other people on my team.

I am always looking for new business.

I practice seasonal objections before the season comes around.

I know how to get myself out of a sales slump.

I don't make excuses.

I love the basics.

I fake it until I make it, if things are not going well.

I listen to audio tapes and read books on sales.

I have my life goals written out in detail and I carry them with me all the time.

I focus on what I'm doing at the time.

I am always working on a better way to communicate something.

I have a great lead tracking system.

I am very organized with my paperwork.

I send out a lot of thank you notes.

I treat people with respect and professionalism.

I stay on the phone until I've succeeded.

Success for me is 100% internally driven.

I am always on the lookout for something to inspire me.

I let the prospect do most of the talking.

Although my results are affected by my self-esteem, I try not to let my self-esteem be affected by my results.

I use my product.

THE SELLING PROCESS

*C*hapter 1

STEP ONE—THE INTRODUCTION

"If it ain't broken, break it!"

—Harvey McCay

*T*he introduction or greeting step is the easiest step of the entire selling process, yet many salespeople, in many different industries, do a poor job of developing the rapport that will last the duration of the visit. Worse yet, most salespeople don't even realize they're doing a poor job and will continue selling with the same bad habits. Perhaps salespeople don't develop their skills on the introduction step because it doesn't seem very important and, after all, they are still managing to close sales so "Why fix it if it ain't broken?"

The truth is that the effects of mistakes made in the initial interactions with prospective members are usually subtle but can be very damaging to the sale and future referral business. In these times of gender sensitivity and political correctness, the introduction step can be a mine field of potential ways to insult your prospective customers.

Below we will take a look at some traditional approaches to this step and make some subtle improvements. See if you recognize some of your own behaviors:

THE INTRODUCTION STEP

Less Effective	*More Effective*
Being too confident when first meeting prospective members. It's no secret that people sum each other up in about the first 30 seconds of meeting. Salespeople often make the mistake of being too enthusiastic and forward with prospects who, in turn, misinterpret the outgoing, confident approach as superficial and canned.	**Approach the person in a calm, nonaggressive manner.** Take a second or two to notice their body language and their level of comfort with the situation. Concentrate on making them comfortable instead of making the sale.

Less Effective	More Effective
Starting with open ended questions or invasive questions. Questions like "So tell me about yourself!" or "How much time have you set aside for your workouts?" can make the person feel uncomfortable with you. Today's prospect is much more savvy to the selling process. Tact and diplomacy are essentials to this step.	**Make it easy for the prospect to be with you and in your club.** Once you have developed rapport you can ask your prospect almost anything, but initially it's important to ask questions that are easy to answer. Ask light questions and listen carefully to their answers. Questions like "How did you hear about the club?" and "Do you live in the area?" are easy to answer and still pertinent to the situation.
Starting the tour right away (without asking questions). Picture the stereotypical door-to-door salesman who immediately opens his case and goes right into his canned sales pitch. This is the mark of the amateur. Starting the tour right away gives all of the control to the prospect. Additionally, you can't really help someone until you know some basics about their needs and wants. This is doubly true for the aggressive prospect who starts out with something like, "I only have five minutes and I want the prices now!" Giving over power and control to this type of prospect will definitely not result in making a sale.	**Take control of the interaction from the start.** You are a professional membership consultant and you have information that the prospective members need in order to make a decision. Inform them matter-of-factly that you will need to ask a few questions and then will be happy to show them around and give them rate information. If the prospect is an aggressive type and is in a hurry simply say, "Actually, it takes about 15 minutes to tour the club and give you the price information you need. Will that work today?" Don't be afraid of losing them. Aggressive people actually respect firm, but not aggressive, boundaries and will usually comply.

Now that we have the preliminaries out of the way it's time to move on to the actual introduction step. This part of the selling process is the only one where I suggest some memorization. Many sales representatives just ask whatever questions come to mind during the introduction. Actually, you will appear much more confident and professional if you ask the same initial questions of every prospect. If you really think about it there is a logic to the selling process and some very logical initial answers you will need before proceeding.

EASY SELLING SCRIPT— THE INTRODUCTION STEP

Ask the four introduction questions below of all prospective members:

"Hello, my name is Brenda. I will be showing you around today." Always shake hands with prospective members regardless of gender or age. Making appropriate physical contact will help you build rapport with people.

1. How did you hear about the club?
This is a must if you want to know which of your marketing efforts are actually creating traffic. Scientifically, we know that a variety of sources can contribute to a visit or a call, but it helps to know which of those sources helped this person take action.

2. Do you live in the area?
Chances are that the majority of your members live or work near your club. If your prospects don't live or work near your club, you may want to ask about convenience. It is better to ask if they live in the area first and save work

details for later in the process. Work-related questions tend to make people feel that they are being qualified financially.

3. Is this membership for yourself?

This tells you what you need to know in order to give them the information they need to make a decision, without the potentially insulting questions about marital status, children, and so on. Never use the words husband, wife, family, or children unless the prospect mentions them first. You really run the risk of making a mistaken assumption during this step. Stay with what you need to know to sell memberships, not what you want to know or are curious about.

4. What motivated you to come in today?

This is one of my favorite questions because it helps to soften the boundaries people have and get them talking about their needs. Something motivated that person to come in today. Some prospects may simply report that they saw your ad in the newspaper, yet others will go right to their needs.

The introduction step is complete. Before you move on to step two, the needs analysis, check the following Make-It-Happen Tips to make sure the club is doing everything possible to make this step a success.

MAKE-IT-HAPPEN TIPS

- **Update your tour and guest registration system.**

The old guest sign-in book simply won't cut it any longer. You need different information from a guest than you need from a tour. Examples of each follow.

The guest book creates unnecessary steps for follow-up calls, and so on. The most efficient way to keep track of guests and tours is to have a registration card. If the card has two copies, one copy can double as a tracking card for follow-up and the other can be kept on file to make sure the club has its own copy of all guests and tours.

- **Train the front desk to get all prospects to fill out the card.**

Ideally, the front-desk person greets the prospective member, asks him or her to have a seat and fill out the (brief) form, and informs the individual that a membership consultant will be with him or her momentarily.

Once the prospective member is seated—and not until then—the front-desk person telephones the sales department and lets someone know that a lady or gentleman is waiting for assistance. This sets the mood of professionalism and formality—two things we really need more of in our industry.

- **Train the sales department to handle the up-system.**

The front-desk person should not have to determine who is next. It is enough to do all of the initial handling of guests and prospects in addition to other duties at the desk. The sales team can track the system behind the scenes, away from the eyes and ears of prospective members. If the sales staff cannot, a problem much bigger than tracking exists.

MAKE-IT-HAPPEN TIPS *continued...*

• **Create an open place to talk to prospects be-fore touring them.**

Offices are out! They make people too uncomfort-able. Most clubs can easily add a table or two with a couple of chairs, or perhaps a couch or two, and some flowers, to the lobby area and have a perfect area for conducting the introduction and needs analysis steps. Restaurants and cafes are also great.

Don't worry about the distraction of members. Pros-pects feel more comfortable out in the open. Teach yourself not to be distracted by the presence of mem-bers, or other traffic. Just focus on the person in front of you and try to make him or her as comfort-able as possible.

THE ATHLETIC CLUB - Tour Registration Card

Date _____

Please take a moment to answer the following questions:

Name _____

Address _____

City/State _____ Zip _____

Company _____

Phone (Hm) _____ Phone (Wk) _____

Check below the areas you are interested in:
❏ Weight Training   ❏ Swimming   ❏ Tennis
❏ Children's Program ❏ Cardio Conditioning ❏ Basketball
❏ Racquetball   ❏ Social Activities   ❏ Aerobics Classes
❏ Volleyball   ❏ Squash   ❏ Handball

How did you hear about the club? _____

Check below the type of membership you are interested in:
❏ Individual   ❏ Couple   ❏ Family   ❏ Corporation   *Thank you!*

_____   _____
Signature   Toured By

(This is the information you want to get from prospects
who come in to tour the club).

THE ATHLETIC CLUB - Guest

Date _____

Please take a moment to answer the following questions:

Name _____

Address _____

City/State _____ *Zip* _____

Company _____

Phone (Hm) _____ *Phone (Wk)* _____

What part of the facility are you using today? _____

Would you like membership information?   ❏ *YES*   ❏ *NO*

Thank you!

(Put your club's waiver and consent information here)

_____   _____
Signature   *Initial of Employee*

Note: some clubs print Guest Registration Cards
in numerical order to keep track of guest fee money.

(This is the information you want to get from guests
who come in to use the club).

Chapter 2

Step Two—THE NEEDS ANALYSIS
A Selling Professional's Secret to Success

*"The difference between failure and success is doing
a thing nearly right and doing a thing exactly right."*

—Edward Simmons

*M*any sales books and tapes mistakenly profess that the almighty close is the most important part of the sale. Perhaps that was true when customers were susceptible to the power of the salesperson's constant closes.

Those days are over (Thank goodness!). We have to develop the right to close via the needs analysis. The bottom line is that if you are a poor closer who performs an excellent needs analysis you will still outsell a great closer who has weak needs analysis skills. Anyone can ask a closing question or put the squeeze on a prospect, but finding out a person's needs takes intelligence and a bit of finesse.

If you are having any common "selling problems" you may find that 90 percent of them can be solved by developing your needs analysis skills. The needs analysis is by far the most important step of the selling process.

Take a look at this list of typical selling problems that may be solved by building skills in the needs analysis step of the sale:

- *I'M JUST NOT CLOSING ENOUGH SALES*—If you are not closing enough sales there is an excellent chance that you are missing key information about the prospect which should be unearthed long before you get to the close.

- *I'M BURNED OUT (OR BORED) ON SELLING/MY JOB*—Getting to know important personal information about your prospect gives the job of selling another dimension. People become more interesting to you; not just another tour. This helps the fight against burnout and boredom.

- *I HAVE TROUBLE DEALING WITH HOSTILE OR AGGRESSIVE PROSPECTS*—Hostile and aggressive prospects often become much more cooperative once they realize that you are focused entirely on them and their needs.

- *I HAVE TROUBLE REMEMBERING SMALL DE-TAILS ABOUT PROSPECTS*—Salespeople who focus on the needs often have an easier time remembering prospect details simply because the process becomes more interesting and memorable.

- *I KEEP GETTING THE SAME OBJECTION OVER AND OVER*—A good two-way conversation will reveal some of the potential objections early allowing you to address them before the close.

Before we develop the needs analysis, you may want to see if you recognize some of your less effective habits of this step and consider some of the suggestions for correcting them:

THE NEEDS ANALYSIS STEP

Less Effective	More Effective
Doing the needs analysis while showing the club. Prospects can't tell you their needs and look around at the same time. Watch your prospects on your next tour. They will be busy looking around and not really listening to you. The tour is not a good time to be asking important questions. You should know their needs before the tour.	**Stay seated until you know their needs.** This should only take one to three minutes. Just flow right from the introduction to the needs analysis. Once they mention a need, that's your cue to transition into the tour step. (This will make more sense when you read the sales script for this chapter on page 20.)

Less Effective	More Effective
Asking interest questions too soon. If you start every sales interaction with "Interest" questions like, "So, what would you like to do here at The Athletic Club?" you will have nowhere to go except to show them the items they mentioned. They may resent, or feel confused by, needs questions once they have told you their interests.	**Save the interest questions for the tour step.** Start your interaction (after the greeting questions) with a good needs question like, "What do you hope to achieve here at The Athletic Club?" This will add a much more natural flow to the conversation with your prospect.
Finishing your prospect's sentences. Anxious communicators often ask a question and then immediately give the prospect a list of possible answers to that question. This bad habit may extend into all aspects of your selling style, however, it's the most prevalent during the early stages of meeting someone. Prospects will sometimes agree, or nod along, with the anxious communicator even though the information is not correct. This gives the salesperson a completely wrong concept of the person with whom they are working.	**Train yourself to wait patiently for the answer to the questions you ask.** Some people are simply more thoughtful before answering questions about their needs and wants. Wait for their answers before speaking! It can be fascinating to actually have a two-way conversation with a prospect.

17

Less Effective	More Effective
Asking questions which could intimidate people. Point blank questions that were the norm in our industry can be very intimidating to prospects today. Even a seemingly harmless question like, "So, are you currently on an exercise program?" can be intimidating coming from a salesperson during the initial stages of meeting.	**Be sensitive to the fitness level of the average person and the feelings of failure they have about their exercise routines.** Remember that the public perception of our industry is that we are all super-fit and that we effortlessly work out all of the time. Save the "exercise program" questions for the personal trainers and focus more on the needs of the person in front of you.
Trying to educate the buyer. There are two problems with salespeople trying to educate buyers: (1) the salesperson is doing most of the talking and (2) a sales presentation is an inappropriate platform for educating people about something as personal as fitness. Unless the prospects directly ask you for advice try to focus on discovering their needs.	**Be very careful about doling out exercise/weight loss advice on the tour.** It's much better to whet the appetite of the person with the services you offer and the programs you have for making sure they get the information they need to meet their goals. Focus your attention on selling the buyer now. Educate the buyer later.

A good way to know if you are doing a good job on the needs analysis is to pay attention to the words your prospects use when they answer your questions. Let's examine some *interest* words versus *needs* words:

The following is a list of some possible interests of your prospective members. You will get these answers when you ask *interest* questions like "So, what's your favorite type of exercise?" or "What kind of activity do you like to do?" *Interests* are of very little interest to a professional salesperson. The pro knows that most health clubs feature the same items and what really counts is what the individual is here to achieve from those interests.

INTERESTS:

Aerobics	Swimming	Running
Walking	Location	Staff
Convenience	Step	Slide
Sculpt	Spinning	Testing
Personal training	Schedules	Tennis
Racquetball	Squash	Yoga
Basketball	Volleyball	Impressive list of members
Parking	Handball	Kids programs

Now take a look at the list of what really counts, what people actually get from the club for themselves.

NEEDS:

Time with family	Time away from family
Weight loss	Feel better
Look better	Self-esteem booster
Better sex	More productive
Cures my loneliness	Competition
Social atmosphere	Motivated by the presence of others
Feeling of belonging	Distraction from pain of divorce or
Something just for me	death of loved one
Part of my job	Celebration of next level in life
Networking	Vacation preparation
Stress relief	Lifestyle change needed
Upcoming reunion	Find a new mate
Train for athletic event	Upcoming nuptials
Pregnancy	Postpartum
Mental illness	Kids are grown and gone
More energy	Doctor's advice/medical problem

Take another look at both lists. Are you getting *needs* or *interests* from the dialogue with your prospects? If you are getting mostly interests at present then what can you do to find out the needs? What are the right questions to ask to get to the needs? I have spent 12 years in this industry developing, through my own trial and error, the answer to that question. It really only takes one good question to find out the need. I have come up with a total of three that work beautifully in our industry. Let's take a look at needs analysis questions:

EASY SELLING SCRIPT
CONDUCTING A PROFESSIONAL
NEEDS ANALYSIS:

1. a) *Margaret, what do you hope to achieve here at The Athletic Club?*

This is my all-time favorite question because it is almost impossible not to give a need for an answer. I also like this question because it suits almost all prospects. It's easy to ask and easy to answer. Don't confuse this with a goal question. Goal questions can be too specific for the sales presentation and can make people feel pressured about exercising. "Achieve" is the key word here.

b) *....and is there any special reason?*

Referring to the response of Question 1a, this question takes you one layer deeper into the needs of this person. It also helps you find the need in those occasional cases when the prospect gives you a generic answer to Question 1a, for example, "Oh, just general fitness." That way when you ask "Is there any special reason?" he or she is more compelled to tell you a need.

2. When would you say was the last time you felt comfortable with your level of fitness?

Note: The average response is 10-15 years ago.

I use this question particularly when things are flowing very well with the prospective buyer and I want to keep them flowing and/or when I have a prospect who is too talkative and won't stay on the subject at hand. This question gets people talking.

Don't accidently substitute the words "shape" or "yourself" for "fitness" because you will surely insult the person. Be careful to gently lead the conversation along by continuing with the following questions:

a) ....what was different then?

This question really gets people to open up because it taps into "their story." You might be surprised by the stories you'll hear. I have heard everything from the difficulty of postpartum depression to the victory of being captain of the football team. Your job here is to listen and encourage the discussion, moving onto the next question.

b) Would you like to get back to that level of fitness or is there a happy medium?

This question, I feel, is our professional responsibility to ask. We don't want to accidently encourage people to try and get back into the shape they were in 30 or 40 years ago. This question brings them back to the realistic possibilities of today, instead of the unspoken pressure of the past ideal. Although some people will want to stretch for or even exceed that ideal, most will have a happy medium in mind.

c) **How often do you think you would need to come down here to get to that level?**

In the "old days" we asked this question directly after meeting someone—too obvious. It's much more appropriate now that we know more of the personal story of this prospect. It is only logical to lead into the "how to" aspect of attaining the new fitness level. This tells you what the person thinks they need for himself or herself. Contrary to popular belief, people DO know what they need.

d) **What do you think you would DO here at the club?**

This is a classic interests question, but it's perfect timing now that we know more about the motivation of the prospect. If you would have asked this at the beginning you would have no where to go. By asking it now it serves as a perfect segue to showing them the club.

Note: The prospects may answer question 2 by telling you they are in the best shape that they have ever been. In that case you simply ask question 1a, "What do you hope to achieve here?"

3. **May I ask, have you ever belonged to a club (health club, spa, fitness center) before?**

This is actually a commonly used question. Be careful not to follow this question immediately with an interest question like, "So, what did you DO there?" or you will have nowhere to go, except onto the tour. You can glean a lot of information from a person's past experiences. Try some of the questions listed below.

Note: If the person has never belonged to a club before, simply move onto question 1a, "What do you hope to achieve here?"

a)   May I ask, which club did you belonged to?

This will tell you if they are still members or not and may reveal that the person has relocated to your city (information you may not have gotten otherwise).

b)   What did you like best about that club?

Remember the answer to this question when you are touring this person around your club to make sure you address this interest.

c)   Was there anything in particular you didn't like about that club?

Note: Avoid the word "gym" as it connotes a lower-level operation than the words club, spa, and so on.

The reason for this question is obvious: You want to hear them verbalize any dissatisfaction with the other club to make sure it doesn't come up as an objection later.

MAKE-IT-HAPPEN TIPS

• **You only need one, or maybe two, needs analysis questions to find out the needs.**

Listen carefully for some of the answers listed above.

• **Don't try to change the subject if you get some very personal stories like the pain of a death in the family or divorce.**

Just listen carefully and empathetically. The person will tell you more if they want to and will stop talking about it if they don't.

MAKE-IT-HAPPEN TIPS *continued...*

• **Be professional and diplomatic when asking needs questions.**

Do not be condescending and patronizing like the dinosaur salesperson of our industry.

• **Take on the mannerisms of a Membership Consultant.**

Be intelligent, informed, articulate and genuinely caring for the client.

• **Take notes if you like.**

Generally, people are flattered and it will help you remember the most important things about your prospect.

• **Needs questions are better asked in person than in writing.**

Some clubs put the questions on the registration card to insure they get asked. This makes the form a bit threatening because it would be too long, and it doesn't allow you to see the body language of the prospects when they answer your questions.

• **Really understand the power of needs.**

Call someone you sold in the last 30 days and ask them what really made them join the club. If they answer "It was because of you or because of the equipment" ask them what else. You will most likely get a need like, "Well, I was just so burned out on the stock market and I really needed something for myself." Go ahead, try it! The answers you get will amaze you.

If you have mastered this chapter then you are well on the way to being a master of the selling process. The rest is easy. In the next chapter we'll examine the easiest part of the selling process, the tour.

*C*hapter 3

STEP THREE—FINE TUNING YOUR CLUB TOUR

"Never miss a good chance to shut up."

—Peter Benchley

*T*he tour step, like the introduction step, is an area that salespeople don't take very seriously when it comes to skill building. The thought is often, "How hard can it be to show the club?" or "Our club practically sells itself."

The tour is the presentation of your product and, done properly, takes a good deal of skill. Besides that, nothing, and I mean absolutely nothing, sells itself these days! Let's take a look at some commonly made tour mistakes and some considerations for change:

Less Effective	*More Effective*
Museum tours! Long tours are boring to many prospects and can be very impersonal. Also, many salespeople go on "automatic pilot" on the tour, giving the same tour to all prospects regardless of their individual needs and interests.	**Customized tours!** After the needs analysis and before the tour, ask the prospects what they are interested in seeing. As you pass an area simply ask if they would like to see or know about that area. This indicates to people that you are listening and paying attention to them.
Listing every feature of each area as you pass it. Congratulations if you have memorized every detail of the club but please don't make every prospect listen to it all.	**Taking the prospect to the area of MOST interest first.** Simply take the prospects to the area of most interest to them, and then ask them if they would like to see other possible areas of interest.
Putting prospective buyers on the equipment during the tour. This is an outdated technique previously used to "involve" the prospects. It actually doesn't sway them either way so why not avoid such an obvious tactic.	**Pointing out the variety of members using the club and equipment.** If you are trying to show people how easy it will be for them to acclimate to your club, simply point out to them all of the different types of people using your club.

WHY SOME SALESPEOPLE MAKE THE MISTAKE OF GIVING LONG TOURS

Some of us get the mistaken idea that the more we show the prospects, the more it will be worth to them—thus, the long tour.

Actually, the opposite is true. People are interested in the areas they will use. They may act impressed with all of the areas you show them but inside they may be thinking, "Gosh, I have to pay for all of this stuff that I am not going to use."

Remind yourself that most of your current members utilize only one or two favorite areas of the club (we wish it were different, but it's not). Those areas are where the value is for them. To pay dues and only swim or only take aerobics is worth it for them, and it will be for the new member, too.

Another reason that some salespeople give long tours is that possibly the tour is the only part of the selling process with which they are comfortable. They start the tour the moment the prospect walks in the door and claim that they can do a good needs analysis on the tour. They have memorized every possible detail about the club and generally tell every prospect every detail every time. For this person the end of the tour means the dreaded close so they prolong that agony as long as possible. At the end of the tour this person often issues a guest pass and skips the close all together.

If the above describes you, you have a little work to do. The first is to read over and over chapters 1, 2, 4 and 5 in this book which focus on the other steps of the selling process. Train yourself to sit down and do a needs analysis in the beginning and to sit back down to present prices and ask the person to join. Focusing your entire sales presentation on the tour is not really selling, it's just touring.

The benefits of shorter tours are many; however, the best benefit will be that you will be talking less and asking more questions. Because questions are key to successful selling you will most likely increase your closing ratio by shortening your tour.

TRANSITION QUESTIONS/STATEMENTS

You will need a question or two to make a transition from the needs analysis to the tour. The transition also gives you a chance to summarize what you have discussed so far—a good habit to acquire. Try something like this:

"Well, Margaret, it sounds like you have come to the right place to help you cope with the new stress of your promotion and relocation. I think you will be really pleased when you see all that we have to offer professional members like yourself. Also, we do open at five a.m., so you can get here before the stock market opens. As far as meeting people and making friends, that should be easy. We have some kind of member event every month. Last night 75 of us went to see a Broadway play. Of course, you will meet some members and staff at the new member orientation which is the first Thursday of next month."

"Now before we tour the club, what do you think you'll do here at The Athletic Club?"

or

"What part of the club would you like to see first?"

TOUR QUESTIONS OR
TRIAL CLOSING QUESTIONS

The reason I use these titles interchangeably is because trial closing is really what the tour is all about. If you have done a good job of asking about needs, listening closely to the answers, and bridging your club to the person's needs, then the actual showing of the club is a minor point. Therefore, the point of showing the product is really best used to get confirmation of where this person is in his or her readiness to make a decision—a.k.a. trial closing. You won't need to ask all of the questions below, just choose a few for each interaction:

1. How soon were you thinking about getting started?

I love asking this question on the tour because it's an honest question and catches people a bit off-guard. Off-guard questions tend to elicit honest (uncensored) answers.

2. How often do you think you'll come down to the club?

A true trial closing question. This question will tell you if the person is planning on joining or if he or she is not yet ready to make a decision.

3. How many aerobic classes will you take per week?

"Aerobics" can be substituted for any aspect of your club. This is the same type of question as number 2. Any good tour has several of these "How many" questions in it.

4. What time of day will be best for your schedule?

Same effect as numbers 2 and 3.

5. Do you prefer to work out on your own or with someone else?

MISCELLANEOUS TOUR QUESTIONS: SMALL TALK WITH A DIRECTION

1. Tell me about your work. Is it stressful?

This will help you find out a bit more about possible needs and will often tell you where the person works so you can see if he or she qualifies for a corporate discount.

2. So do you think you'll join?

One of my favorites. This one needs no explanation.

3. What is the most important consideration for joining a club?

4. Have you lived in the area very long?

Note: The answer to a tour question is your cue to match what you hear with what the club has to offer. This keeps the conversation natural and informative at the same time.

TWO QUESTIONS YOU SHOULD NEVER ASK A PROSPECT

1. What do you think?

There are so many better questions than, "What do you think?" Ask a trial close, or better yet, a closing question. Ask about the weather but please don't ask, "So, what do you think?" It puts the prospect on the spot and feeling pressured.

2. Do you have any more questions?

Another weak question. Ask a specific question instead of stalling before the close. Anyway, if you're a professional you have been asking most of the questions, not them.

EXAMPLE OF SURPRISE PRICE DROPPING

"Okay, Margaret, this is the main aerobic's studio. We have more than 60 classes per week for you to choose from. Because you are an early morning person you can choose from the six a.m. classes on Monday, Wednesday and Friday, or the 6:15 classes on Tuesday and Thursday. Mary teaches in the morning and she's excellent. Once you take a class here you'll notice the special suspended floor is very giving, that will help you while your knee is healing. In the other studio we offer yoga and Ti Chi classes in case you can ever get in during the evenings or weekends. Our instructors are all certified and we have all of the wonderful gadgets like slide, the workout bands and balls to keep classes interesting. **Margaret, your monthly dues would be only $61, and we do have an enrollment fee which I will explain when we finish touring.** Now, off to the locker rooms. Do you like to steam or sauna?"

THE PRICE-DROPPING TECHNIQUE

I accidently discovered this technique after I had been selling in our industry for about six years. I was getting a little bored with the selling process and started "tweaking" with the basics of selling—a bad habit of veteran salespeople. I was so confident in my closing ability that I started surprising prospects by telling them the prices on the tour. It worked great!

I have since discovered that "surprise price-dropping" works great with any type of product. Here's how it works:

Step One: Take the prospects to the area of most interest to them first.

Step Two: Describe the area in detail according to what you know will interest them.

Step Three: Drop the rates nonchalantly (dues only, save the enrollment fee for later).

Step Four: Change the subject immediately and continue the tour.

KEYS TO SURPRISE PRICE-DROPPING

There are three reasons why this technique works:

1) It's a surprise—giving you, not the prospect, control over when you discuss the prices.

2) It is information they want to know anyway.

3) Your casual approach to the rates makes them sound very do-able. This significantly reduces the pressure that comes with quoting the rates at the end of the interaction.

Be certain to quickly change the subject after dropping the price or the prospect will feel compelled to ask more price-related questions. A small percentage will anyway, don't sweat it. Just answer a few questions and tell them you will go into more detail after the tour. Avoid any out-of-date or indirect comments like, "All this for only one dollar a day." If you have several rates it's best to choose the highest one because you can always go down in prices, but you will never convince someone to spend more than you initially mentioned.

MAKE-IT-HAPPEN TIPS

- **Try to avoid group tours.**

It's very difficult to do a good Needs Analysis on groups of people who are not related. If possible, it's better to focus on one prospective buyer at a time.

- **Avoid taking pages or interruptions during the tour.**

You are with someone who deserves your full attention.

- **Train sales staff on entire selling process—not just tours.**

If non-sales staff personnel, such as M.O.D.s, fitness staff, and so on, are going to do tours, make sure they are trained in the entire selling process, not just how to tour. Your club will usually not get another opportunity with that prospect. Use it well.

- **Take all of the extra energy you now have from shortening your tours and put it into prospecting (Chapter 7).**

Chapter 4

STEP FOUR—PRICE PRESENTATION AND CLOSING
DIPLOMACY AND TACT MAKE A GREAT COUPLE

"We are what we repeatedly do.
Excellence, then, is not an act but a habit."

—Author Unknown

*P*resenting the rates to the prospect and asking for his or her business are two steps that go hand-in-hand. I cannot think of one circumstance when the two should be separated. For that reason I like to treat them like one very important step. Of all the steps in the selling process this is the one that seems to give salespeople the most trouble and discomfort. It's pretty obvious why salespeople are uneasy with this step because they have to talk about money.

Adding insult to injury, most of the sales training books and tapes focus on the easiest part of this step, the closing questions, and do nothing to help salespeople eloquently and diplomatically discuss the rates and money with their prospective buyers. Let's take a look at some common habits of the Price and Close Step and some good replacement behaviors:

Less Effective	*More Effective*
Handwriting the prices as part of your price presentation. This out-dated technique, which was the hallmark of our industry in the 1980s, now serves as an immediate Red Flag to prospects who have been "pitched" in this manner in the past. The fact that the technique is now used by most multi-level marketing organizations (a.k.a. pyramid schemes) should be reason enough to avoid it.	**Have your published rates printed in an attractive manner.** Have a nice rate card or sheet printed and use that to present the rates to people. If you are concerned about the rates leaving the building, simply have the one card made for each office and have them laminated. Feel free to cross off published rates in front of prospects and write in discounted rates you are offering at the time.

Less Effective	More Effective
Presenting more than two, or three at the most, membership options. Your membership options shouldn't be a built-in reason for people to "go home and think about it!" Some of the rate sheets I've seen are absolutely mind boggling. There is no reason to present off-peak, temporary or short-term memberships to prospective buyers unless they have directly indicated their interest in such a membership.	**Select and present the membership you feel is the best option for that individual.** You can always present the other types if the one you presented doesn't suit him or her. As long as you are honest and you have the person's best interest (in fitness and finances) in mind then you can do this without worry of deception. You are a "membership consultant," and you should know best which membership suits your prospects.
Overwhelming the prospect with too much information at the close. There is no reason to blither on too much about cancellation and billing policies and procedures or any other unnecessary details (For example, "Now, Margaret, in the event you want to quit the club you will need to notify us in writing by mail or you can deliver it to the accounting office which is located on the second floor. If you quit, we will issue you a temporary card and use up the dues you pre-pay today, of course, assuming that your account is clear with us. Now onto your billing...").	**Touch on the club policies and procedures but focus on the close.** This is not to suggest that you avoid important details at the close, just that you don't overwhelm your prospect in the name of "full disclosure." Once the person has made his or her decision to join, you can take out a checklist and go over each detail. He or she will listen much more attentively at that point.

Less Effective	More Effective
Avoiding your club's idiosyncrasies altogether. This is the opposite of overwhelming the prospect with details. Don't avoid talking about known idiosyncrasies (like Electronic Funds Transfer (EFT), 30-day cancellation notice, and so on.) because it will seem like you are trying to hide it or apologize for it. Get comfortable with the way your club does business and never apologize for any aspect of your club.	**Build idiosyncrasies into your presentation.** "Now Margaret, the way we handle billing is through electronic funds transfer from your checking account or credit card. You will find 100 percent of our members do it that way. Do you prefer credit card or checking?"

THE PRICE PRESENTATION

Ninety-nine percent of the salespeople I have trained needed work polishing their price presentation. A polished price presentation has the following components:

- Smooth and uninterrupted delivery
- Committed to memory
- Without ums, ahs and ohs
- Delivered while making eye contact with the prospect
- Not too fast, not too slow
- Contains customized points that are important to that prospect
- Delivered without nervous habits (touching hair, mouth, rocking, etc.)
- Said with confidence and comfort with the rates
- Ends with a closing question

EXAMPLE OF A POLISHED PRICE PRESENTATION

"As I mentioned on the tour, Margaret, our monthly rate is $61. Our enrollment fee is $200 and that is paid one time only. Your membership includes complete use of the entire facility including speciality classes like Yoga and Ti Chi. You will find all of the personal amenities you need are in the locker room such as shampoo, conditioner, body lotion, and so on. We will issue you a daily locker and towels are free of charge. All you have to bring is yourself.

"Here is a fee card for extras like massage and tanning. You are welcome to put those on your account if you would like. We would like to enroll you for your personal fitness evaluation as quickly as possible. If you have never had one, you will be amazed by the quality of the information you will get about your personal exercise needs. All of our members pay by electronic funds transfer from a checking account or credit card. If you are serious about joining, you have come at the perfect time because our enrollment fee is 50 percent off. That will save you $100. Shall we get you started?"

CLOSING QUESTIONS

A closing question, such as the one above, always, always, always follows the price presentation without hesitation or exception:

THE OPTIONS CLOSE

Would you like the executive or the sport membership?
or
*Are you leaning toward the couple or
the individual membership?*
or

*Would you prefer to have your EFT
by checking or credit card?*
or
Do you prefer to pay monthly or annually?

THE DIRECT CLOSE

The only thing left to do is the paperwork.
or
Let's get you started.
or
Shall we get you started?

THE URGENCY CLOSE (after quoting full price)

*If you're serious about joining, you've come at
the perfect time* (now quote discounted prices).

Be careful not to give away the surprise of the discount by saying "Our normal rate…" or "Our published rate…", implying that it is "different" now. Instead, quote the full rate, continue on with your presentation, and then use the urgency close. This will have much greater impact on the buyer if price is an issue.

THE ASSUMPTIVE CLOSE

*Okay, here we go. Just go ahead and fill this out
and I will get your temporary card started.*
or
If you step over here we'll get your photo taken.

THE PROCESS CLOSE (my personal favorite)

Joining The Athletic Club is a very simple process. First you will need to complete the application, then we'll talk about how you'd like to pay, get your photo taken, and you'll be all set to go. Would you like some coffee?

or

(for prospects short on time)

Joining The Athletic Club is a very easy process. First this quick application. Then you can pay by credit card or checking. We can take your picture later and you'll be out of here in 15 minutes. Coffee?

At this point the person will either indicate to you (verbally or non-verbally) that he or she would like to join–in which case you want to complete the necessary paperwork and inquire about friends or colleagues who may be potential members—or he or she will voice a concern or objection. Before you move on to handling objections, congratulate yourself. You have asked someone to buy. Presenting and closing alone is more than half of the battle!

POINT OF SALE REFERRAL GENERATION

To make things simple and easy, try this method after clearing membership paperwork:

"Margaret, as a special gift for joining, we would like to offer you a complimentary one-week pass for one of your friends or colleagues. If you would like to write your friend's information in the space provided, I will be happy to arrange for him or her to see the club and will issue him or her pass at that time. Sound good?"

Now what's so hard about that?

MAKE-IT-HAPPEN TIPS

• **Presenting and closing in an office is not necessary.**

With some practice, you can do it in the lobby, cafe or open area. Your prospects will be much more comfortable with the process if other people are around.

• **Have your presentation packets ready.**

Just a plain folder with a membership application, class schedules and perhaps a newsletter will do in a pinch. Be prepared to present without having to dig through drawers or piles.

• **Keep your rate card simple and elegant.**

Try to remove all of the unnecessary information and disclaimers.

• **Consider eliminating some membership options if you have more than three.**

Less is more when it comes to membership options.

• **Get comfortable with the rates and fees.**

Think of the hundreds or thousands of members who happily pay the rate your club charges. It's worth it to them and it will be worth it to your new members.

*C*hapter 5

STEP FIVE—ADDRESSING BUYER CONCERNS AND OBJECTIONS

"Winning isn't everything—it's the only thing."

—Vince Lombardi

*A*ny sales professional knows that buyers experience a bit of buying pain or hesitation. Some people, like me, only experience the buying pain for a split second and then out comes the checkbook. Others experience the pain of indecision for months, even years. Most of your prospects will fall somewhere between those two extremes.

The true sales professional does not take objections as a personal reflection of his or her selling skills, but as a natural, and even welcome, part of the selling process. Furthermore, any sales professional who has been selling awhile in our industry knows that all of the objections we get pretty much boil down to the same thing: Fear of failure.

Regardless of what people actually say, most are in some way afraid that they won't reach the goals they have set for themselves. Therefore, joining a club will be a waste of time, money and effort.

With that in mind, let's take a look at some classic bad habits during this step and easy replacements for them:

Less Effective	*More Effective*
Using needs analysis information to "brow-beat" prospects. This outdated technique is where the salesperson takes information gained in good faith from the prospect and uses it to make the prospect feel guilty or foolish for objecting (For example, "Gee, Margaret, I am surprised that you need time to think about it since you said you really wanted to lose the weight you gained after your last baby.") This tactic is insulting and unprofessional.	**Ask a good question to help you re-establish rapport with the prospective member.** (For example, "Margaret, I can certainly understand your wanting to give it proper thought and consideration. May I ask, what are the aspects of the club you will be thinking about the most?")

Less Effective	More Effective
Offering a trial membership or guest pass instead of addressing the objection. Even if the person came to your club in response to the offer of a trial membership, you still need to address the objection at hand. Offering a visit robs you of the best opportunity to deal with the customers' concerns while you have them in front of you.	**Get in the habit of selling people without the crutch of offering a free visit.** A fair amount of your prospective members don't even expect a free visit but would love to have one if you offer it. There is nothing wrong with giving a trial visit if that is how the person heard of your club, but invariably a number of people are ready to join today!
Turning a prospect over to another salesperson or manager. This dinosaur tactic is popularly referred to as the T.O. Most automobile salespeople throughout the United States still use it. Need I say more?	**Do your best to address the objection and then end the interaction on a good note if you are unsuccessful at selling them on the first visit.** When you feel you have done the best job you could at persuading someone to join, there is nothing wrong with ending the interaction, scheduling a time to talk again, and walking the person to the door, treating this individual just as you would someone who had joined that day.
Aggressive, inappropriate or point-blank questions. (For example, "You must not be serious about your goals if you are going home to think about it," or "Do you think your husband would have an objection to you feeling better about your body?" or "Aren't you ready to do something about your shape?") This is another old technique borrowed from the '80s.	**Empathetic, appropriate and professional questions.** The great news is that you can be even more effective without the use of antiquated, pushy selling tactics and feel better about what you do for a living. Questions like, "What did you have in mind, regarding your schedule, when you first decided to visit the club?" will feel much better to everyone involved.

THE FIVE STEPS TO OVERCOMING/ ADDRESSING ANY OBJECTION

1. RELAX — Sometimes our discomfort with this part of the selling process is obvious to our prospective buyers. Train yourself to just relax and to expect objections from people after the close.

2. REPEAT THE OBJECTION OR PARAPHRASE FOR UNDERSTANDING — The main reason for this step is that it gives you a moment to compose yourself and quickly recall your strategy for this objection. The wonderful side effect is that you make people feel as if they've been heard when you repeat what they said.

3. SHOW EMPATHY VERBALLY OR NONVERBALLY — This little split-second step has the job of reconnecting you with your prospect. The prospect is unconsciously waiting for you to be disturbed by their objection. Not only are you not disturbed, you're empathetic.

4. ASK A KEY QUESTION OR MAKE A KEY STATEMENT — This is the most important step. The key question or statement should not be inappropriate or insulting. So what's left? Plenty of well-timed, strategic questions and statements that will help move the prospect out of the objection and into one of three positions: 1) into another objection, 2) into a yes decision or 3) into a no decision.

5. CLOSE AGAIN USING A SOFT CLOSE OR GUARANTEE CLOSE — You'll know when it's time for this step because you have a sort of awkward feeling and may wonder, "What's next?" The re-close is next.

Let's go through some objections. As you read through see if you can figure out where each step starts and ends. The key questions/statements are in bold. Obviously, I cannot demonstrate Step Three for you in this book, but don't forget to use it. Empathy is the foundation of addressing objections:

EASY SELLING SCRIPT—BASIC OBJECTIONS

1. I need to talk to my spouse.

"So, you would like to go home and talk with your spouse? Well, that certainly makes sense. What do you think he'll say?" Just ask the question and pause. Don't answer for her.

a) Oh, he'll be fine with whatever I decide.

"Well, perhaps then you would like to go ahead and get started. If you are okay with it, I can take your check and details and hold the paperwork until morning. That way, you can go ahead and talk with your husband. Just call me in the morning and tell me to process it or not."

b) He will have a major problem with it!

"What will you do?" Again just ask and wait. Don't attempt to advise, just listen and respond. She will tell you either that she'll join anyway, in which case you have the sale, or that she won't.

2. I would really like to look around at other clubs.

"So, you would like to have a look at other clubs? Well, I can understand that. May I ask, of all the clubs you want to see, which one are you considering the most?"

This will help you narrow the competition down so that you can comment.

THE DOWNTOWN ATHLETIC CLUB

The key here is an honest, articulate appraisal of the competition. Never use sarcasm or insults when speaking of a competitor.

"You know, Margaret, it is part of my job to know about all of the clubs in the area. The D.A.C. is a very nice club. They have a beautiful swimming pool, which we do not. The main difference for you is that they don't have nearly the aerobics program we have. Nobody can really compete with our three large studios and the quality of instruction we have. Also, you will find their dues are about $10 per month higher. If you are leaning toward joining our club, you might consider going ahead and joining and then, of course, by law, you have three days to get over to the D.A.C. and make sure you joined the right club."

3. It's too expensive.

You can't address this objection until you clarify.

"So, you feel that it is too expensive? May I ask, is it the monthly dues or the enrollment fee that is too expensive?"

4. It's the enrollment fee.

"So, you are okay with the $61 per month, but feel the enrollment fee is too high?"

"Yes. If you could just waive that I would join right now."

"Thanks for letting me know. It may help you to understand exactly why we have an enrollment fee."

Select from one or a combination of the following responses:

- "It's a one-time fee. You won't have to pay that again."

- "Everybody pays an enrollment fee here. We just don't waive it. It is just how we do business."

- "We put your money right back into the club. For instance we just added $20,000 in cardio equipment to our fitness center to make sure that our members won't have to wait for equipment. That's not something you find in other clubs."

- "Not everyone can afford an enrollment fee. This way you are joining a club that needs less members overall and has a rather exclusive clientele."

Avoid telling the prospect that the enrollment fee will be used toward his or her fitness evaluation or starting program as he or she may choose to skip that procedure and demand a lesser or waived enrollment fee. My favorite combination is of the first and third responses.

"If that makes a little more sense to you we can go ahead and do your paperwork. "

5. It's the dues.

"So, you are okay with the $199 enrollment fee but you feel that the dues are too high?"

"Yes!"

"I see. May I ask how often would you need to come down to the club in order to justify the $61 per month?"

When someone says the dues are too high we translate that into to value and cost justification. The prospect is wondering if they are going to get his or her money's worth.

"I don't know. About four times per week, I guess."

"So, you would like to get down here four times per week?"

What you are doing here is walking the person back through the process to help him or her see that they probably do have a plan for getting his or her money's worth.

"And you were thinking aerobics during the week and weights on the one weekend day you come in?"

"Yes."

"You know, Margaret, you sound like you have it worked out in your mind. Four times per week would help you get well on your way to achieving your goals. You are here today and you seemed pretty excited about getting started. If you would like, we can go ahead and start your paperwork."

6. I'm afraid I just won't use the club.

Refer to 5 above. This objection is handled exactly like the objection to the monthly dues. If you already covered everything in 5, try number 7 below.

7. I don't know if I will have the time to use the club.

"So you don't know if you have the time to actually use the club?"

"Right. I am really busy and I'm just starting on a new project at work."

"That's understandable. I can only imagine how busy you must be running a law firm like you do. May I ask, when you first came in to see the club today what did you have in mind as far as how you would handle your schedule?"

People almost always have a good answer to their own dilemmas. They just forget temporarily. Be careful to sound respectful, not condescending.

"Well, I was figuring at first I would just get in after work, twice per week until I finish the project. When things get back to normal I can come first thing in the morning."

"Margaret, that sounds like a pretty good plan. You sound like so many of our members when they first joined. At first, it's hard to imagine how you are going to fit it in. Later, it's hard to imagine how you ever lived without it. It's up to you if you would like to wait, although it sounds to me like you are ready to get started. Shall we?"

8. I need to think about it. I never buy anything without thinking about it.

"So, you would like to really think about joining the club?"

"Yes."

"Well, that is certainly understandable. May I ask, when you are home pondering the club, what aspects of the club will you be thinking about the most?"

"Probably the..."

The prospect will usually tell you another objection at this point. Once you have it isolated simply start the process over, addressing the new objection, dues, enrollment fee, my spouse, use, time, and so on.

9. Look, you have a nice club here but I am thinking about joining that super cheap club down the road from here.

"So, you are considering joining the XYZ club?"

"Yes. I know it's not beautiful like here, but I don't need much. I just need a place to work out."

"Well, it makes sense that you want to get the best price for what you want. You know, Margaret, you may want to consider a few things while making your decision. There is no question that you get quite a bit of equipment for very little cost over at XYZ Club. One thing you have to keep in mind is that their lower price leaves very little barrier to entry. That means that anybody and everybody can join that club. For you, that will translate to waiting for equipment, possibly being turned away from aerobics classes, less than clean facilities and a much less mature group of members than what you would have here. The XYZ club is that price for a reason. I can promise you that we will never be that price. Our members would not be so loyal if we had that many members here. It really depends on what you are looking for. Once again, if you are leaning toward joining here I will be happy to get you started. Of course, you have three days to make certain that you want to join."

(The money-back guarantee would work much better here, see page 60).

Take time to memorize each of the basic objections and the key questions that will help you re-establish the rapport with the prospect. You will find that most people give an objection and, when asked about it, will usually give another. Don't panic. Objections are a true signal of seriousness on the part of the prospective buyer.

DETAIL OBJECTIONS

Detail objections are when the prospect hooks into one aspect of your club like parking, location, equipment, and so on, and uses it as an objection. Detail objections *cannot* be overcome at the end of the presentation. It's far too late and would only result in an argument.

If the prospect says, "The club is too far away from my home." What can you say? "No it's not!" That would be an argument, besides you'd never win.

If you are getting detail objections then you need to study up on your needs analysis (Chapter 2). You may be talking too much and missing small, but important details about your prospect. If you knew this was a deal-breaking issue earlier, you would have a better chance of addressing it or cutting the visit short.

COMPLICATED OBJECTIONS

Sometimes the prospect will give you what seems like an overwhelming and very complicated objection, which is just a function of what he or she is feeling. Don't get hooked in by it. Just relax and, above all, empathize. Your mind will sift through the confusion and find the logic of the situation if you just listen. Try something like this:

EXAMPLE OF A COMPLICATED OBJECTION

"My wife just had a baby. There is no way I can join a club like this because she can't come down here. She will kill me. She's already mad because I am working too much and there's just no way."

"Wow, I can only imagine how overwhelming it must be. I also know how refreshing it would be for the two of you to get in here, like you mentioned earlier. Even if it's for a steam or massage. What did you have in mind, as far as your wife and son, when you first decided to come in?"

"Well, I was thinking it would be great for both of us. We get no time alone and she never gets out of the house."

"Do you think you would be able to find someone to watch the little one once a week until he's old enough to use our day-care center?"

"Well, maybe. I was thinking my mother could watch him."

"So your mother could watch your son and you and your wife could get in and use the club together. You know, Mr. Raynes, a lot of our members start out this way, not knowing how they'll fit it in. You came in today. It sounds like you and your wife could really use a break. Would you like to go ahead and get started?"

Complicated objections can sound impossible to address at first. They are almost always filled with personal problems and issues. Don't let that distract you. Listen carefully for the real objection and address it calmly and with true empathy.

OFFERING A MONEY-BACK GUARANTEE

The money-back guarantee is the perfect re-close after going through this process. Avoid mentioning the guarantee until you actually get an objection. You then address the objection and when you re-close, you offer the guarantee. You may find it will increase your first visit closing ratio by 50 percent. Another benefit of the guarantee is that it reduces the number of frequent passes given out to prospects who would join today if they had a guarantee. The guarantee re-close should sound something like this:

"Margaret, you may be pleased to know that we offer a seven day money-back guarantee here at The Athletic Club. What that means to you is that you go ahead and join today, we will process your funds and paperwork just like a full-fledged member.

"This will give you a chance to (insert objection: think about it, talk to your husband, see another club, and so on) and make sure you made the right decision. Does that make you a little more comfortable?"

Be careful not to make the guarantee sound like a no-obligation trial membership. It's not a trial. It's a membership with a money-back guarantee.

Congratulations, you have completed Section 1 of this book, The Selling Process. If you already use this type of selling system (needs based) in your daily selling interactions, you can count yourself in the top 10 percent of professional salespeople. To further define your skills, get ready to work on mastering the incoming call.

MAKE-IT-HAPPEN TIPS

• **Commit the key questions to memory.**
Practice will make you comfortable with the whole process.

• **Maintain eye contact with the person during this step.**

• **Relax and allow your mind to find the real issue the person is facing.**

• **Keep a list of objections you get and study them after the person has gone.**

RESPONDING TO INCOMING BUSINESS

*C*hapter 6

MASTERING THE INCOMING CALL

"Do the thing and you will have the power"

—Ralph Waldo Emerson

$\mathcal{P}$robably one of the most challenging and difficult aspects of selling in the health and fitness industry is handling the incoming call. I don't know if you've already noticed this but either you're really good on the telephone or you're really ineffective on the telephone.

When you're selling in person, things like your appearance or the way that you shake hands and all of those in-person factors come into play to really help you connect with the person. You don't have any of those things going for you on the telephone. It's purely telephone skill.

The main goal of taking incoming calls is that you can eventually book 70 percent to 80 percent of your calls to appointments, and those appointments are showing up 90 percent of the time. A lower ratio will adversely affect your total sales for the month because the majority of prospective buyers will place an informational call prior to visiting the club. So if you are not at that point yet where your bookings (or conversion ratio) are high enough you will get a lot out of this chapter. If you are already booking 80 percent, then perhaps you will make use of some of the words, phrases and methods outlined.

First, let's take a look at telephone selling habits and some possible areas for change:

Less Effective	More Effective
Giving prices or a price range over the telephone. My research over the years has shown that clubs that quote rates and ranges over the telephone get lower overall appointment bookings. We'll get into this further in this chapter, but you can test it for yourself. Not giving rates is harder, but it is also more effective.	**Wait for an appropriate time (not right off the bat) to tell the caller that you simply don't quote rates over the telephone.** Assure the individual that you are reasonably priced and invite him or her in to see the club. Confidence and control are key factors here. See script on page 72 for more help.

Less Effective	More Effective
Listing the features of your club on the telephone. If you catch yourself blithering on the telephone about all of the features, measurements and detailed aspects of your club's features you are probably just a bit nervous about being on the phone with prospects. No human could possibly absorb all of the detailed information you give him or her about your club. Listing all of the features on the telephone may be boring your prospects instead of booking them.	**Ask questions about the caller's interests.** When he or she gives you an interest like "aerobics" tell them a little information about that area like, "Judy, we have more than 60 classes per week and excellent instructors." Then invite him or her in or ask another question.
Closing for the appointment too quickly. If you are having a lot of no shows (more than 25 percent) on your appointment book, you may be closing too quickly. Many new salespeople start asking people to come in and see the club the moment they pick up the phone because they are uncomfortable with the process and want to end the call as quickly as possible. You need to build a little interest before someone is going to come and see you—especially if you are not going to answer their price questions.	**Start closing for the appointment after you have heard some of their interests and told them a little information about the club.** Use statements like, "We have a very popular squash program and have seven international courts, the best thing to do is to come down and see the club for yourself. How does your evening look?"

Less Effective	More Effective
Ignoring the prospects' request for prices or trying to change the subject. We did this in the '80s but it doesn't work any more. Prospects are more sales savvy now and they know whether or not their questions are being addressed.	**Address the issue of prices BEFORE the prospect has a chance to ask again.** After asking a few interests questions, take charge by saying something like, "Margaret, you asked about our rates. We actually don't quote our rates over the telephone. What I CAN tell you is that our rates are reasonable and competitive. The best thing to do is come and see the club for yourself. How does your day look tomorrow?"
Letting the caller ask all the questions. In almost any conversation, the person asking the questions is the one in control. You need to be asking most of the questions.	**When the caller does ask a question, address it and then ask a question yourself.** Be careful not to pause too long or they will ask another question. Know your telephone script and have your questions ready when you take the call.
Asking for the person's telephone number or address unless you have an appointment with him or her. Having the prospect's telephone number or address is pointless unless you have an appointment set up. You can not do anything with that information. You will get very little response from follow-up calls or mailed information from a prospect with whom you couldn't book.	**Focus on the number one goal of the incoming call— to get an appointment!** The telephone number, last name, day-time phone and all that information will surely follow but first you've got to focus on getting that appointment.

THE PSYCHOLOGY OF THE INCOMING CALL

So now the telephone is ringing and you are about to take the incoming call.

What you need to understand about this caller is that despite what they say and despite what you think, they are interested in purchasing your product or a product similar to it. Something emotionally has triggered them to pick up the phone and you need to have empathy and understanding in your voice and at the same time maintain complete control of the conversation.

If you take a position that you're just there to give information and answer their questions and let them get off the phone as quickly as possible, you're going to have a lot of difficulty booking the incoming appointment. This is where the mastery comes into play.

It also helps to keep in mind that the callers don't really know what they want. They know they're interested but they don't know how to get information from a business that really sells something intangible. This is why 99 percent of the callers will ask the price over the telephone. They don't know what else to ask. Your job is to help them understand what their club needs are, how your club can meet their needs, and why they should come down to see that club as soon as possible.

EXCELLENT REASONS NOT TO QUOTE RATES OVER THE TELEPHONE

• If you really listen carefully you'll notice a lull in the conversation after giving the rates to the caller. The lull occurs because the person doesn't know what to do next. He or she doesn't have enough information but they don't know what else to ask. If you have control over the conversation, there will be no lull.

• Quoting a "price range" often annoys the prospect further because a little information makes him or her want all of the information, NOW.

• Unless you offer the lowest price in town, people will generally think that your club is overpriced when they hear the price without having seen the facility.

• People tend to make their decision solely based on price once they are quoted rates over the telephone.

• Quoting the rates over the telephone will actually lower the number of calls you successfully convert to appointments as well as the number of people that actually show up for their appointments.

EXCELLENT REASONS TO CONSIDER GIVING RATES OVER THE TELEPHONE

• The persons have seen the club recently. If I were relatively certain that they had indeed seen the club then I would go ahead and discuss rates with them. I would also ask them to join after quoting the rates because that is the logical next step (see Chapter 4 for closing questions).

• If your club is the lowest price in town then there isn't much harm in telling the callers the rates. Personally, I would tell them that we have the lowest rates in town and that they should see the club, and still wouldn't quote rates. But, you can go either way.

TAKING THE INCOMING CALL

"Membership, this is Brenda, how may I help you?" Answer the phone with enthusiasm. State your name and always be focused, without distractions, and ready to handle the call.

Step One: Deflect the price inquiry with reassurance of information to come. "I'd be glad to give you some information. I need to get a little information from you first."

Step Two: Take control of the conversation by asking pertinent questions.

Select from the following questions:

1. How did you hear about the club?

You have to know that sourcing information for marketing.

2. Have you seen the club before?

This communicates to the prospect "Oh, you want pricing information but you haven't seen the club before."

3. Is this membership for yourself?

Avoid using the words husband, wife, family or children unless they do first, as you may insult someone. Just to be safe, you always ask: "Is this membership for yourself?" or "Are you interested in membership for yourself?"

4. What are you interested in doing here at The Athletic Club?

To this answer you will match some of the club features to whet the appetite for a club visit.

Listen attentively to the answers to the previous questions. If you give out a little information make sure you follow it with another question.

Step Three: Maintain control of the conversation by addressing their request for rates (preferably before they ask again).

"Margaret (or Ms. Jones), you asked about rates earlier, actually we don't discuss our rates over the telephone. What I can tell you is that our prices are reasonable and competitive with other clubs in the area. The best thing for you to do is come on down and see the club for yourself. If you are looking for a club in this area you will really want to see The Athletic Club."

Note: Whenever you talk about rates, whether you give them or you don't, the basic rule in sales is never, ever pause. If you pause, that prospect will have a wide open space to move right in and ask you specific questions like "I only want racquetball; how competitive are you with other clubs in the area?"

Move quickly to the next step.

Note: If your club is not competitive with other clubs substitute the second sentence with the following:

"What I can tell you is that we are an exclusive club and very reasonably priced for the value that we offer our members."

Step Four: Ask for the appointment (close).

"When would be the best time for you to come in and see the club? Are mornings or evenings better?"

Of course, you always want to give at least two options when booking an appointment. Try to book the appointment within 24 hours of the call so that they can see the club while their interest is still high. However, you don't want to give them the impression that the calendar is wide open either. Give people the impression that things are busy, people are seeing the club, people are coming in.

Step Five: Book the appointment.

"Okay Margaret, that's 2 o'clock tomorrow afternoon. And what is your last name? Your daytime telephone? Evening phone in case I need to reach you? Can I give you directions to the club? Again my name is Brenda. I am certainly looking forward to meeting you and I'll be waiting at the front desk for you at 2."

Step Six: Confirm 100 percent of your appointments.

"Margaret, I am very much looking forward to seeing you at 2 o'clock. Do you have good directions to the club?"

If you have an appointment in the morning, you want to call them at home the evening before, otherwise the day of the appointment is fine. Be very assumptive in your confirmation because if you leave the smallest opening like, "I was calling to see if you're still coming at 2 o'clock" or "I'm calling to confirm the 2 o'clock appointment" and then pause, you run the risk of them canceling.

HANDLING OBJECTIONS ON THE TELEPHONE

Without question, you are going to get certain telephone objections. The objections will come when you are attempting to book the appointment. I recommend that you memorize these responses. Otherwise, the prospect will catch you off guard and you'll lose the chance to book the appointment.

TELEPHONE OBJECTIONS

Objection	Response
Thank you for the information, I'll have to think about it.	I can understand that. You know, John, you may have more to think about when you come in and see the club first. Let's go ahead and schedule your tour; that way you can decide for yourself. The phrase "decide for yourself" is very important and powerful and you'll want to use it often, both personally and on the telephone.
I'll have to check with my husband (wife) and get back with you.	That's understandable. Why don't we go ahead and schedule you tentatively, you can get back with your spouse tonight and we'll confirm tomorrow or reschedule if that doesn't work. Was morning or afternoon better?

TELEPHONE OBJECTIONS

Objection	Response
I'm just too busy; I'll have to get back with you.	I can understand that. You went ahead and called today so let's just schedule you and it'll take ten minutes to see the club. We'll give you the information that you need so that you can decide for yourself.
There's no way I'm coming in to see your club without prices!	Sir/M'am, I can certainly understand your frustration. Our thinking is that if someone is really interested in our club, he or she will take the ten minutes to come in and see the club. I can assure you, whatever you decide, it'll be worth your time to come and see the club. When is the best time for you? You're siding with their frustration by saying "I know you're frustrated, I know this is hard for you to understand."
It's probably too expensive if you won't tell me what the rates are.	I think you'll find it very reasonably priced. Really, the best thing to do is to come down and see the club for yourself.
But I got this mailer that said you offer $100 off the initiation fee. How much is the initiation fee?	Yes, we are offering $100 off our initiation fee and I'll be more than happy to go over those details with you when you come in to see the club. When is the best time for you?
Well, I'll just drop in sometime this week.	We give tours by appointment only, that way I will definitely be available for you and you won't have to wait. When would be the best time for you to come in?

HANDLING THE OBNOXIOUS CALLER

I am chuckling to myself as I write this section as it just occurred to me that most other industries don't get obnoxious callers. I don't know what it is about us that makes about one out of every ten callers go buggy, but it does happen.

Let's get a few things straight before we proceed:

• Potentially obnoxious callers usually refuse to give you their names or any information about themselves.

• Not all callers to your club are obnoxious. Don't confuse demanding callers with obnoxious callers. Most people are demanding these days.

• Your tone is everything. Remain calm throughout the interaction.

• Warn the caller that you will put the telephone down if he or she is using profane language. If the profanity continues, go ahead and hang up (gently).

• You can often downgrade a person from "obnoxious" to "demanding" by the way that you handle him or her. Conversely, you can just as easily upgrade a "demanding" caller to "obnoxious" if you have poor telephone skills.

• Don't feel bad or guilty for losing an obnoxious caller. Just mark it on your tracking report and move on.

This type of caller has to be handled in a specific way. It's very important that you don't judge all the callers by this standard. The worst thing that you could do is to handle all of your incoming calls this way. That would be unnecessary because only one or two out of ten can be defined as obnoxious.

HANDLING THE OBNOXIOUS CALLER'S REFUSAL TO GIVE YOU HIS OR HER NAME

"Actually, Sir/M'am, we have a policy here at our club that we don't give information out unless you're willing to give us a little bit of information first. Like I said, my name is Brenda and your name is?"

Often they will give you their name at that point. Otherwise, it is pointless for you to spend time on the telephone with somebody that won't even give you his or her name. You run the risk of spending five very tenuous minutes on the telephone with them and they end up hanging up on you anyway.

HANDLING THE OBNOXIOUS CALLER WHO CONTINUES TO PRESSURE YOU FOR PRICES

"Sir/M'am, you should know that we are a privately owned facility and we simply choose not to divulge our pricing information over the telephone. As I said, we are very reasonably priced and very competitive with other clubs in the area. The best thing for you to do is come down and see the club for yourself."

If they persist:

"Sir/M'am, we could go on and on like this but the bottom line is that we just don't divulge our price rates over the telephone. I really hope that you can come on down, take ten minutes to see the club and I'll give you all the price information in person. That is just the way that we prefer to do business." Be careful not to use phrases that will further annoy people. "We're not allowed to give rates" is going to put you in a position of weakness possibly making the caller even harder on you. Another phrase you want to avoid is "It's our policy not to give rates over the telephone." "Policy" is a loaded word and generally people do not respond well to it. Stay calm and try to understand their frustration.

MAKE-IT-HAPPEN TIPS

- **Make sure that the incoming call is routed properly when it comes in to the club.**

Finally, a precious incoming call is created by your savvy marketing efforts. Make sure it doesn't get fumbled. I recommend that you take the "up system" away from the front desk staff (mentioned in Chapter 1, The Introduction). They have enough to do. I realize that this creates some logistical questions for the sales department but it really is the responsibility of the sales department to handle the "up system."

- **Try to have a separate space for making and taking calls.**

You don't ever want to take an incoming call in front of a prospect or a member. It's tacky and unprofessional. There is a strategy to taking incoming calls and members or prospects should never overhear them.

- **Set up a productive telephone environment. This goes for incoming and outgoing calls.**

It should be clean, well lit, free of debris and motivational to those who use it. Ideally, this would be out of the view of members; that would allow the team to hang posters or motivational sayings to keep them going while making and taking calls.

MAKE-IT-HAPPEN TIPS *continued...*

• **Get a headset (if possible). The cost of electronic headsets has gone down dramatically in the last few years.**

Your telephone productivity will soar. It allows your hands to be free and has a microphone that comes to the mouth. Besides keeping your neck from getting sore from being on the phone most of the time, it frees you up to comfortably speak with the prospect and you may find that your ratio of booking incoming calls to appointments is increasing.

Note: You may want to develop hand signals to alert your co-workers when you're wearing the headset so they can tell if you're on or off the phone.

• **Stand up.**

It makes you stronger and more powerful.

• **Learn to project enthusiasm, sincerity and attentiveness on the telephone.**

Some-times you don't feel so great about being on the telephone and that affects how you come across on the telephone. Remember, you're going to lose at least 50 percent of your enthusiasm through the telephone line. You'll want to project even more enthusiasm on the telephone and it will come across to the prospect as just average enthusiasm.

• **Discuss only positive interactions.**

If you have a bad interaction on the telephone, try to forget about it.

• **Track all of your calls.**

You have to know your ratios if you want to master the selling process and the incoming call. (See tracking form and ratios figuring format on the next page).

SUCCESS TRACKING SYSTEM

Representative Name _____   Week of _____ Through _____

	1 Incoming Calls Today	2 Appointments I Booked from 1	3 Walk-In Tours Today (No. Appt.)	4 Membership Sold to Walk-Ins	5 Set Appointments in My Book Today	6 Actual Tours from Appointments	7 Appointment Sold Today	8 Be-Backs (previously toured) Sold Today	9 Outbound Telephone Contacts	10 Appointments Generated via Outbound Activity	TOTAL SALES TODAY
M											
T											
W											
TH											
F											
S											
SU											

Sources (Tick a source for any call-in or walk-in)

Member Referral _____
Non-Member Referral _____
Corporate Referral _____
Coporate Letter _____

Yellow Pages _____
Newspaper _____
Club Event _____

Direct Mail Piece #1 _____
Direct Mail Piece #2 _____

SUCCESS TRACKING SYSTEMS

Ratios for the week of _____ **through** _____

If you have 7 calls in column 1 and you booked 5 appointments in column 2 you would divide the 5 by the 7. Your incoming calls to appointments ratio would be .714284714 or 71 percent.

1. Calls to appointments
   divide 1 into 2 or 2 / 1 _____

2. Walk-ins to sales
   divide 3 into 4 or 4 / 3 _____

3. Tours to appointments or
   no show ratio
   divide 5 into 6 or 6 / 5 _____

4. Appointments to sales
   divide 6 into 7 or 7 / 6 _____

5. Be-backs to total sales
   divide total sales into 8
   or 8 / total sales _____

6. Outbound contacts to
   leads divide 9 into 10
   or 10 / 9 _____

GENERATING YOUR OWN BUSINESS

*C*hapter 7

PROSPECTING AND FOLLOW-UP
A HIDDEN GOLD MINE FOR EVERY SALESPERSON

*"You have in your composition a mighty genius
for expression which has escaped discipline."*

—H.G. Wells

Salespeople are generally pretty independent people. We don't like the feeling of depending on others very much, especially when it affects our income. When I was a sales rep in a club, I became very frustrated when the club's marketing didn't go well or when marketing dollars were short and the telephone wasn't ringing enough. I developed my own follow-up and prospecting systems out of frustration. I wanted to have more power and have control of my income.

My position on membership salespeople cold calling is that it is unnecessary if you take advantage of the gold mine that surrounds you. If you want to sit around waiting for incoming calls and walk-ins, then you may have to resort to using the telephone book to generate some business when you are short of your goal.

However, if you choose to be independent, instead of dependent on the marketing ability of others, then you simply have to make a daily habit of prospecting and follow-up calls.

Let's examine the three areas easily available for prospecting and follow-up:

1. The guest pass call
2. The referral call
3. The follow-up call

THE GUEST PASS CALL

This call is to guests who have visited the club. My research over the years has shown that about one-third of your guests are true prospective members. It is a bit disappointing isn't it? We want to believe that everybody who comes into our club is a prospective member, but it's just not true. The other two-thirds will not even consider joining your club for a variety of reasons. This information should cause you to take two actions: 1) collect guest fees from the two-thirds who will never join anyway or 2) get in touch immediately with your guests to find the one-third who are possibly interested. Additionally, you may want to ask the question, "Are you interested in membership?" on your guest waiver. That way you will know who to call first (see example in Chapter 1).

The actual call is easy. I find it's best to just get right to the point:

"Hello, this is Brenda Abdilla from The Athletic Club. You were a guest in our club last week and I'm calling to see if you'd like to have some membership information?"

The call can take three general directions:

1. Guest says that he or she is interested.

Go right into your script for the incoming call (e.g., "Great, is this membership going to be for yourself? Do you live in the area? What kinds of things are you interested in?"). (See Chapter 6 on the incoming call.)

2. Guest says that he or she is not interested, but doesn't sound sure.

Ask a few questions (e.g., "Is there any special reason? Do you belong to a club presently?").

3. Guest says that he or she is not interested and sounds angry or irritated.

Thank him or her very much for his or her time and end the conversation.

Move on to your next call.

THE REFERRAL CALL

These calls are incredibly easy, pleasant and can reap great rewards. Simply take the list of names from any sales month and give each person a call to offer them a complimentary trial membership for one of their friends. Try this approach:

EXAMPLE OF A REFERRAL CALL

"Hello, Margaret, I'm calling to make sure you're comfortable at the club. We have a special gift for you for having recently joined the club. We have made special arrangements for you to invite one of your friends to join you here at the club for an entire week, with our compliments. Your friend will have complete access to the club during that time. If you would like to go ahead and choose someone, I will call him or her and arrange a tour of the club at which time I will issue his or her one-week pass. Sound good?"

Ideally this would be said at point of sale; but this will cover you just in case.

THE FOLLOW-UP CALL

Of all calls, this is the one sales representatives dread most. You have toured the person recently and for some reason he or she didn't join. Now it's time to call and, and, and, say what? Therein lies the problem. What do you say?

It's easy, really, but first let's look at what not to say:

- Avoid asking the prospects what they thought about the club. This is an odd question, and it puts the prospects on the spot and it makes them feel pressured.

- Avoid starting off the conversation with a close. It's a little bit too abrasive and it's too strong to start off a conversation.

- Don't ask the prospects if they have made a decision yet. If they had, and it was yes, you would know about it.

- Don't attempt to readdress an old objection such as, "I'm calling to see if you've had a chance to talk to your husband yet." The prospect will just make more excuses.

THE GOOD NEWS CALL

This call is based on the assumption that most people respond positively to the thought of receiving good news. The other assumption is that if they don't respond to good news, they probably won't respond to anything.

I adapted this idea from the "Good News Message" in a seminar lead by Jim Smith, president of Peak Performance magazine. If you don't happen to sell a prospect on the first visit, get in the habit of making some notes about him or her on the back of the prospect card. That way you will have some information to use when you call to follow-up with some good news. Try this:

"Hi Joan, this is Brenda Abdilla; I'm calling from The Athletic Club. I have some good news. We have extended the day-care hours on Saturday to 6 p.m."

People will generally pause here. That's your cue to move into an invitational-style close.

"Well, Joan we would love to have you as a member of the club. Shall we schedule a time to take care of the paperwork?"

The good news can really be anything. It doesn't even have to be something new. You can even mention information you may have missed on the tour. The key is that the good news opens the conversation and lays the foundation for your follow-up.

OTHER GOOD NEWS CALLS:

"Joan, I have some good news. We are offering a free personal training session to new members right now. That way you can start off right. I think you will love the club. Should we set a time?"

"Joan, I have some good news. Our outdoor volleyball court opens next week. You mentioned you wanted to be outside more. We'd love to have you as a member of the club. Can we schedule a time for the paperwork?"

If you get the person's voice mail or answering machine, simply leave a message stating that you have some good news and leave your telephone number. Be sure you have a special file so that you can retrieve the information quickly when they call you back.

MAKE-IT-HAPPEN TIPS

- **Move past procrastination, get on the telephone, and stay on the telephone.**

Telephone avoidance represents a fear of rejection. Get yourself to move past the fear by setting some goals (e.g.,"I'm going to make 20 follow-up calls today and five referral calls.").

- **Relish in the occasional incoming call.**

You can expect a lower level of interest from the outgoing calls you make, in comparison to incoming calls.

- **Use momentum to your advantage.**

If you're having a good day on the telephone or a good month in sales, use that to your advantage. Get on the phone and stay on the phone.

- **Never start out a telephone call with someone you don't know by asking "How are you?"**

It's a Red Flag that you are selling something.

- **Be selective about making calls at the right time.**

Don't use this advice as a reason to procrastinate, but be aware of the ideal times to make calls in your area.

*C*hapter 8

ADVANCED PROSPECTING
CAPTURING THE CORPORATE MARKET

"He who has begun his task has half done it."

—Horace

$\mathcal{N}$o topic in our industry generates more conflicting information. This has caused me a great deal of frustration as a sales trainer as I have to spend more than half of my entire corporate sales training time debunking all of the myths and misinformation out there.

Actually, once you tear away all of the junk information and properly adjust your expectations, you may find working with the corporate market to be incredibly easy and even enjoyable. It allows membership consultants to stretch their skills a bit and creates a pleasant change of pace in the everyday life of selling.

'CAPTURING THE CORPORATE MARKET' DEFINED

The corporate sales effort is really defined as internally marketing your club to people at their workplace or place of common interest. This may be a restaurant, bank, car dealership, Fortune 500 company, Chamber of Commerce, church, medical office, insurance provider, real estate agency, and so on. The point is that if you can gain access to this group of people with a compelling enough tool, you are more likely to get their business as individuals and as a group than any other effort available to you.

We will examine how to quickly gain access to decision makers as well as the best tool to use once you're in. But before all the fun begins, let's take a look at those myths:

MOST COMMON MYTHS ABOUT CORPORATE SALES

• Company decision makers are interested in the benefits of fitness.

This will change, hopefully very soon, but for now it's just not true. The fact is that companies don't really care about fitness and don't care to hear us babble on about all of the benefits of exercise or the boring studies done to support these facts. They know the benefits of exercise better than we do in most cases because it is part of their job. However, they don't and won't care until it directly, unquestionably, affects their bottom line.

• The best companies to call on are the largest and the ones that are closest to our club.

That's just not true. Owners of clubs tend to think that because a company is across the street from your club, you should be able to get 10 percent or 20 percent of the employees. If a thousand people are there, you should be able to get 100 to 200 memberships. It's just not true. It's good math and it's good thinking and it's hopeful but it just doesn't work like that.

You may have a car dealership that has nine salespeople and a manager and you may sell memberships to all ten of them. Conversely, you may have a Fortune 500 company with 5,000 employees right next door to you, and sell only two or three memberships from that company.

Essentially, the size of the company and the proximity to your club doesn't matter. What does matter is that if we play our cards right, we will be able to market to a number of people at once because they all work in the same building.

- If the company purchases the membership then both sales and retention will be better. Company-paid memberships can actually have a higher attrition rate than those of individuals. The company decision makers usually have unrealistic expectations for club use and may not want to continue paying once they see the real average usage rate is only once or twice per week, at best.

Think your individual prospects will sign up quicker once the company agrees to pay? Also not true. A Minneapolis-based company agreed to purchase memberships from me for its 28 vice presidents. The only problem was that in the 90-day sign-up time I could only get eight of those V.P.s to actually join. I tried going to their houses, their offices, everything; they just simply weren't interested. It doesn't make a difference who pays for the membership.

Our goal is to go in there and get memberships without spending a tremendous amount of money on external advertising. Sponsorship is not necessarily the goal. Of course, if the company wants to pay, we'll take it but that's not the number one goal.

- The best approach to targeting a company is to find a contact and work your way up through the company, through that person.

Dangerous mistake. Once you have initiated contact with someone inside the company, you are taking a risk by going above his or her head. He or she may sabotage your internal marketing efforts. The best way to approach a corporation is to start at the top and work your way down, if you have to.

- We have to talk the language of corporations with proposals, attractive brochures, videos and formal presentations.

I spent countless hours putting together proposals and presentations for company decision makers who would never agree to see me. If you can't get in to see the decision maker, it doesn't really matter what kind of material you have. If you can get in to see the decision maker, and you will, you won't need any of the above to get what you want.

• We have to be good negotiators.

You will rarely be in a position that you have to negotiate price for memberships. One or two times per year, a corporation will approach you regarding what you can do for its employees. In that instance, you should get the owner or general manager (someone in addition to yourself) to negotiate together. The rest of the time you will be marketing to the individual inside companies, not really negotiating.

THE TOP THREE GOALS OF WORKING WITH A COMPANY/GROUP

1. To extract the maximum possible number of individual memberships from that company

We have to get it out of our heads, finally, that we're going to go into some business with a briefcase and calculator in hand and we're going to come out with 50 memberships. It just doesn't work like that. A few times a year, you may get a couple of groups of memberships, maybe 10 or 20 or 50 or maybe 100, depending on your club. The rest of the time, when that's not happening, you can do so much with the corporate marketing effort.

2. Develop a first name basis relationship with a key decision maker

The benefits of this can pay off in a number of ways. Primarily, you have someone at the top who can give you carte-blanche access to market to the entire organization.

3. Exposure of the physical club to the group

The benefits of this are obvious. The more people who see the club, the better the chance of increasing memberships. Many clubs are willing to do too much in the name of "exposure." So be careful to make sure one of the other goals is met in addition to this one.

Before spending your money, time or other precious resources with a company or group, make sure your efforts meet at least two of the top three goals. Three out of three is even better.

TITLES OF KEY DECISION MAKERS TO TARGET

President or Owner	Chief Finacial Officer
Managing Director	Chief Executive Officer
Vice President	General Manager

A WORD ABOUT HUMAN RESOURCE DIRECTORS

You may have noticed that the human resource director was not listed above. This is the most controversial issue that I deal with in my corporate sales training programs.

We tend to want to go the path of least resistance. The fact is, you can get through to human resource people. They will take your call and they'll take the appointment. So what's not to like?

This person has a great deal of power and no decision-making ability. A potentially deadly combination for someone trying to market within that company. It took me countless efforts to learn this truth.

If possible, you will get a lot further with a person who has power and decision-making ability. It is important to remember that human resource people exist to create equity throughout the company. Your club may not be a product for everyone. Perhaps only the top people can afford it. Do you think your human resource contact is going to support that?

H.R. directors will, more often than not, sabotage your internal marketing efforts. Try starting at the top. If you absolutely cannot get through, then try the human resource director.

GETTING PAST ADMINISTRATION

A general manager I once worked for said to me, "Why can't you sell memberships to all of these presidents and vice presidents around here? Why don't you just invite them all to lunch here at the club and I will sell them myself?" The problem the G.M. didn't understand was that if I could get the attention of a company president or V.P. I could sell them myself. Without lunch! The problem was getting past the force field of their administrative assistants.

Try these methods that I have fine-tuned over the years:

Let's assume the president of that company is James Dixson. When you call, you're going to try to get past administration so that you can speak directly to James Dixson. One of three things is going to happen:

1. The person in administration is going to answer "Bronson Industries, how can I help you?" You're simply going to use the decision maker's first name and you say "Jim, please?"

   This method will work approximately one-third of the time. You'll get through because that person is busy, or that person is at a switchboard, or that person is a busy assistant to someone and has many things to do simultaneously. We want the administrative assistant to think that, maybe, you know Mr. Dixson personally.

2. The secretary may return your response with "Who's calling please?" You simply give your first name.

   Again, it's based on the same informality as above. This will work approximately another one-third of the time.

   As you can see, your task of getting through to the decision maker will be quite easy about two-thirds of the time. The remaining third will take a bit more finesse:

3. The assistant does a "full-on screen" and says "May I tell him what this is in regard to?" Don't panic or hang-up. Just relax and find a clever way to exit the call. There are two important goals to achieve when exiting the call: a) never give up your name and b) don't say or do anything that

will cause the administrative assistant to have a negative response to your call (they may not know your name, but they will remember your voice).

Don't be tempted to work through the administrative assistant to market your club; you will get approximately a 90 percent failure rate. Try some of these exits:

Is he not in?
or
When will he be available?
or
I have another line ringing. I will phone again later.

Try calling back early in the morning when the decision maker might be working alone, or call back in the evening. Another tactic is to try at lunch when you know somebody else is covering that particular post.

SPEAKING TO THE DECISION MAKER

You will want to be psychologically prepared when calling a company because chances are excellent that you will get right through to the decision maker. The method I use has been fine-tuned over the past 14 years and it works better than any other internal marketing method I have tried. Read through it and see what you think:

"Hello, Mr. Dixson, this is Brenda Abdilla calling from The Athletic Club. I won't take but a moment of your time. The reason I'm calling is that we have made very special arrangements for all of your employees and their families to have a complimentary one-week pass to our facility." (Expect a pause here).

"Now, Mr. Dixson, instead of simply issuing the actual passes, we'd like to put the complimentary pass information in the form of a brief letter to your employees." (Another pause).

"What I'd like to do is stop by your office for 10 or 15 minutes. I'll bring an information packet on the club and we can work out the details of the letter at that time. How does your Friday look?"

If you haven't noticed, the vehicle you're using is the one-week trial. Let's put it up against our top three goals and see how it does. Does it extract individual memberships out of companies? Yes.

TIPS

- Commit the script to memory—it has been tried and tested

- Speak clearly and not too quickly

- Avoid any type of small talk with this person

Does it develop a relationship with the top decision maker? Absolutely; you've got a 10- or 15-minute appointment with him or her. Does it expose the maximum number of people from that company to your club? Absolutely.

The benefits of using a trial as a marketing vehicle to corporations are endless. One of the best benefits is that the calls come directly to you, the membership consultant. Your name is on that letter and people call you directly to arrange their pass.

Other benefits include: the trial has value, it is something people want, the letter and so on, are easy for the decision maker to say yes to, the trial will get you a 15-minute audience with a key decision maker, and you are reaching every employee of the company with a vehicle that costs the club nothing. If you follow the previous script and tips you will get approximately a 90 percent yes rate on distributing a letter throughout the company. You may get an objection. Let's deal with any possible objections from the decision maker.

POSSIBLE OBJECTIONS

Objection	Response
(Distribution) We don't allow outsiders to distribute information to our employees.	I can understand that, Mr. Dixson. You may want to reconsider this one, however, because this is not a solicitation. It's a gift to your employees valued at (name a value here).
(Unacceptable method of distribution) Why don't you just bring those letters down and we'll put them up on the bulletin board or we'll put a stack of them in the lunch room?	I appreciate the offer. The problem is our owner is very fussy about our image and would not take well to seeing our company on a bulletin board. In order for us to be able to give your employees the free trial to our facility, we would need the company to arrange individual distribution. Ideally, a payroll insert or perhaps a placement in their individual mail boxes. Does that sound okay?
(Too busy) You know, Brenda, this sounds great, however I don't have time to visit with you for the next four months.	Mr. Dixson, that's so disappointing because if I can get in to see you within the next week, we can have their letters out to them by the first of next month and that way the employees will have the entire month to chose from. I could come very early or very late in the day if that is more convenient for you.

POSSIBLE OBJECTIONS

Objection	Response
(Talk to someone else) Brenda, this sounds excellent. Let me put you through to John, our human resource director, and he'll take care of it. We'll be happy to distribute the letter and I thank you for calling.	Mr. Dixson, for the very first time we do this, I need to have the approval from you. In the future, I'll be more than happy to deal with John. Sound good?

BEFORE YOU GO

- Always confirm the appointment. You can do this through the administrative assistant.

- Call back and get directions from the receptionist or the switchboard. Don't bother the decision maker with this.

- Always arrive early. You will have yourself in a frenzy if you're late for a key appointment with the decision maker. It's very hard, as we all know, to get yourself out of the club. Plan in advance, get there early.

- Call in advance to collect your preliminary information. You can ask the administrative assistant how many years they've been in business, how many employees they have, is this their home office, all of the small but important details that will make you feel more informed.

- All you need to take with you is a briefcase with the information packet that you promised, calculator (maybe), your business cards and a pad of paper and pencil.

VISITING WITH THE DECISION MAKER

This is the most exciting part of the entire program. You will find people will treat you very well, even in the largest of corporations.

There are two goals to the visit: 1) to find out if the company is interested in purchasing memberships, and 2) to arrange distribution of the letter. I suggest that you take this list of questions with you and ask the same questions every time:

1. Mr. Dixson, of your 238 employees, how exactly do they break down?

In other words, how many managers, how many administration? The reason that you ask this question is because perhaps later they'll be interested in purchasing memberships only for administration staff or only for the attorneys of a law firm. So, you want to know how this breaks down because it may help you at a later date.

2. Mr. Dixson, what benefits do you currently offer your employees?

You will get a variety of answers to this question. The reason we ask this question is we want to see how generous the company is. If it provides a number of employee benefits, maybe it would consider sponsoring memberships in the future. If it provides the absolute minimum, maybe the chance is not as good.

3. What is the company's position on fitness?

Basically, we want to point blank the decision maker on exactly where it stands as far as fitness and wellness is concerned. You'll get a variety of answers here. It doesn't matter what the answer is, your job is to just find out where the company is.

4. Mr. Dixson, would you ever consider sponsoring memberships for your employees?

You may be surprised that the answer to this question is "no" 90 percent of the time, and they'll tell you why. That's the reality with which we're dealing. We tend to think that 50 percent of the companies are interested in memberships and that's not true. So what are you doing there? Just wait, you'll see.

5. Hypothetically speaking, Mr. Dixson, if you did sponsor memberships, what would be your number one reason for doing so?

Make sure you pause after this question because you will get a very informed answer. He will either tell you that he would do it because it would reduce absenteeism, improve morale, improve productivity or because it's an excellent perk for his employees. He knows the reasons and the benefits of exercise.

Maybe in the next six monthes he remains uninterested but in the six monthes that follow that, he becomes mildly interested in purchasing memberships.

Now you know what the company's main need is because you've gotten it from the top. So, if you're going to do a proposal or presentation, at least you know what approach to take.

Thank the decision maker for answering your questions and move on to the details of the letter. Show him or her an example of the letter you would like to use and find out necessary details for customizing it like: How do they refer to their employees? How will you date the letter? Does it need to be folded? This is also the time you will discuss distribution.

Ideally, you will put the letter on the company's letterhead because that will have more credence with the employees; and ideally, you will put it in with the paycheck. A lot of companies have gone to electronic payroll so this may not work. Find out if you can individually distribute that letter to the employees in some way. Don't settle for just a newsletter insert because you won't get a very good response. A newsletter insert in addition to a check insert would be great.

You may not realize this yet, but one of the major benefits of the visit with the decision maker is that he or she has the power to help you market the club to his or her company. The reason they will help you is because they feel guilty. In psychological terms this is referred to as "The Law of Reciprocity."

The decision maker thinks that you came in specifically to get him or her to sponsor memberships and he or she said "no" to you and that he or she has turned you down. What he or she doesn't realize is that they can do many other things for you. You can activate the "law" by asking one final question:

"Before I go, is there anything that you can think of to help promote this week of fitness during the month? "

This is where you can really maximize your marketing efforts within that corporation. Here are just a few possibilities:

- Reproduce the entire letter in their newsletter.

- Allow you to come during their lunch hour and set up a booth or table.

- They ask you for a proposal.

- They allow you to attend a meeting with five to ten top decision makers.

- The decision maker uses the pass.

- Lunch.

- The decision maker gives you a list of names and numbers to personally follow up with.

- Mail the letter to their homes at the company's expense.

MAKE-IT-HAPPEN TIPS

- **When designing your letter, keep it simple and elegant, not a sales pitch for fitness.**

Explain the offer, list some of the features of your club and how they can reach you to arrange their visit. I suggest dating your letters at the beginning of the month and place an expiration date for the end of that month.

- **If you don't have the names of key decision makers in companies that you want to target for the letter, simply call the company (anonymously) and tell administration that you want to send a letter to the president and need his or her name.**

You don't have to give a reason, just ask for the name.

- **Give your best effort to dealing mainly with the decision maker at the company you are targeting.**

If you simply cannot get through, move down the ladder.

MAKE-IT-HAPPEN TIPS *CONTINUED...*

• **Develop your telephone skills.**

Know exactly what you want and get to the point.

• **Commit to visiting, in person, the key decision maker.**

There are so many benefits to visiting with that decision maker.

• **Avoid resorting to cold calls or unannounced visits.**

This is a waste of time

• **Resist the temptation to quote health and fitness statistics to key decision makers.**

• **Dress and conduct yourself professionally.**

SOME CORPORATE MARKETING IDEAS TO RE-CONSIDER

A VIDEO

The cost is $5,000 to $25,000 to produce. My feedback to you on this is that it's not a good use of time or money. My clients who have done a video have said they're glad they did it but when I ask them if it has generated more memberships for them, they say "no." They generally can't get through to the decision maker to even show the video. That makes the video pointless.

Some logistics make it a bad way to spend your money. For instance, what if the company doesn't have a VCR? If you look at the criteria, it really doesn't meet any of the three goals of working with a company. It doesn't create individual memberships, get you in to see a decision maker, or expose the club to a number of people who wouldn't otherwise see it.

FORMAL PROPOSALS AND PRESENTATIONS.

If you're spending time doing a formal proposal or formal presentation, to whom are you presenting? If you can't get past administration and into the decision maker, then proposals are not a very good use of your time. The key with proposals and presentations is if a company asks you for a presentation, go to that company and ask them some key questions, find out what the needs are and what the budget is and then put together a brief proposal based on that information. If they don't ask, don't bother.

ON-SITE AEROBICS AND EDUCATIONAL SEMINARS.

I used this one to the hilt until I figured out that it's a very good secondary source of marketing but not a very good primary source of marketing. If you get paid on commission, then you want to focus on things that are primary sources of marketing.

LAVISH BROCHURES AND PRESENTATION PACKETS.

I get a lot of questions in seminars and from clients on this. So much effort and valuable time and money go into creating these, which a key decision maker rarely reads.

SELLING CORPORATE FITNESS EVALUATIONS.

This is when you go into a company and sell them, for a certain price ($30, $40 or $60), a fitness evaluation. When I tried this, they sold them like gangbusters. The employees actually came into the club for their fitness evaluation.

Naturally, one would assume that a good number of people would convert to members. We sold a lot of fitness evaluations that year, but it didn't sell any memberships as a result. I would recommend that you do this, but take the salespeople out of the loop so they can continue selling. Again, it's a secondary, not primary, source of marketing.

A BUSINESS EXCHANGE PROGRAM.

That's where you invite companies from the area to come and set up a booth and exchange business cards and tell each other about each others' business. It's a little bit of a money maker but it doesn't sell any memberships. This is something you should do as long as you're not counting on it to create memberships for you. Ideally, have someone else in the club put this together, someone who is not a paid salesperson.

CORPORATE GAMES PROGRAM

You invite companies to compete against each other. It's very good exposure and a lot of trouble to put together. However, it is not the best use of your corporate salesperson's time. Do it, but let others run it.

CORPORATE PARTIES

I've tried this one over and over and over again. We would invite hundreds of people from local companies and nobody would come. It wasn't worth the effort. I suggest you keep this rule in mind with corporate parties: If they host it, they will come; if you host it, they won't come. In other words, if you are down the street from IBM and they decide they want to have a gathering or meeting, be prepared and willing to offer free food. Because the company set it up, the employees will come. One exception to this rule is in pre-sales. You attract more people to your corporate parties during pre-sales; maybe because they think they're going to get a discount. Try to set up the party through the company and have them invite people to your club for some type of function. However, if you're having success with this, there's no use in changing it.

I'm sorry to take all of the fun away. These ideas may be good ideas for a number of reasons. However, they are not the best way to increase memberships. In most cases, you can simply assign the task to a non-sales staff person and the issue is solved. I personally tried them many times, in different ways, before realizing that they weren't resulting in enough memberships to justify all of the time and attention I was giving a prospect.

"*Man's mind, once stretched by a new idea, never regains its' original dimensions.*"

Oliver Wendell Holmes

Index

I

M

N

O

P

ALSO FROM BRENDA ABDILLA...

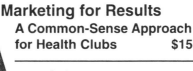

Marketing for Results
A Common-Sense Approach for Health Clubs $15

Softcover, 170 pages
ISBN 1-878956-62-0

Highlights include:

* Top 10 marketing Mistakes
* Smart marketing tactics
* Referral programs that work
* The four-hour marketing plan
* Design Tips

A MUST FOR HEALTH AND FITNESS PROFESSIONALS INTERESTED IN INCREASING THEIR CLUB'S MEMBERSHIP!

AUDIO TAPE SETS

MANAGING SALESPEOPLE - *The Strategy and the Art*

• Motivating & Inspiring Salespeople • Making Sales Meetings Soar
• Tracking & Reporting Systems • Coaching & Discipline
• Hiring & Keeping A Winning Team • Incentives & Compensation

4 Audio Tapes plus Workbook - Only **$139**

CLUB SALES

• Addressing Industry Objections • Goal Setting & Motivation
• Closing More Sales • Questions for Finding Needs
• The Tour & Pricing Step • Selling in the 90's

4 Audio Tapes plus Workbook - Only **$129**

TELEPHONE FINESSE

• Demand for Prices on the Phone • Follow-up Calls
• Refferal & Guest Pass Calls • Prospecting Tips
• Booking the Appointment and Keeping It • Prospecting

2 Audio Tapes plus Workbook - Only **$79**

BUILDING CORPORATE SALES

• Getting Past Administration • Easy to Implement, Successful Approaches
• Most Common Corporate Mistakes • Increasing Your Corporate Market
• What Works & What Doesn't Work for Corporations

3 Audio Tapes plus Workbook - Only **$99**

Order all 4 sets for only $395!

To Order Toll-Free call: 1-800-285-1755
Outside of the U.S.: (908) 225-2727
Or to Order by FAX : (908) 225-1562

CBM Books Order Form

To order by mail, complete and return the form below.

Title		Qty.	Subtotal
Selling For Results: The Health Club Guide to Professional Selling	$19		
Marketing for Results: A Common Sense Approach for Health Clubs	$15		
Managing Salespeople 4 Audio Tapes & Workbook	$139		
Club Sales 4 Audio Tapes & Workbook	$129		
Telephone Finesse 2 Audio Tapes & Workbook	$79		
Building Corporate Sales 3 Audio Tapes & Workbook	$99		
Managing Salespeople, Club Sales, Telephone Finesse *& Building Corporate Sales* All 4 Tapes Sets & Wookbooks	$395		
Add applicable sales tax (CA, CT, IL, ME, NJ, NY, PA, TX)			
Handling Charge			**$1.50**
Shipping: $4 for the first book, $1 for each additional book. Outside of the U.S., please call (908) 225-2727 for shipping information.			
Total Order			

Name_____

Title_____

Company _____

Address _____

City _____ State_____ Zip_____

Country _____

Telephone (____) _____ Fax (____) _____

Payment Enclosed $_____(payable to Cardinal Business Media)

Charge to: ☐ [MasterCard] Mastercard ☐ [VISA] Visa ☐ [American Express] American Express

Account #: _____ Exp. Date_____

Signature _____

Mail to: CBM Books
SFRB0496
    c/o Whitehurst & Clark
    100 Newfield Ave.
    Edison, NJ 08837

CBM BOOKS
Cardinal Business Media Inc.